What's Being Said About Bibby and His Work

"Bibby has become something of a Canadian institution." *-Montreal Gazette*

"He writes with no jargon or professional pretense. Bibby knows a wider readership probably than any other Canadian sociologist."
-Kenneth Westhues, Sociology,
University of Waterloo

"Bibby's always provocative in his take on Canadians' habits and changing ways. He keeps the phones ringing."   -Bill Good, CKNW, Vancouver

"Bibby is rapidly becoming the closest thing to a 'pop sociologist' we have in Canada. He stands head and shoulders above the likes of Decima and Gallup because he proceeds to add flesh to his skeleton of survey statistics."
-Quill & Quire

"He has the unique ability to take his ideas outside of the academic setting. and communicate them with clarity and feeling."   -Cyril Leavitt, Sociology
McMaster University

"Bibby's books are not only packed with information; they also make for extremely enjoyable reading."   -Ann Petrie, *Newsworld*

"Bibby attempts to bring highly technical discussions down to concrete levels. He's one of Canada's foremost popularizers and synthesizers of complex data."   *-Calvinist Contact*

"He does so many surveys I don't know when he has time for anything else!"
-Peter Gzowski, *Morningside*

"One of Canada's leading experts on social trends."
-Tom Harpur, *Toronto Star*

"One of North America's most respected researchers."
-Doug Todd, *Vancouver Sun*

"Canada's premier church watcher."   *-The Hamilton Spectator*

"The closest thing Alberta has to a prophet."   -Ted Byfield, founder,
Alberta Report

"Some church people probably wish Reg Bibby would go away."
-Bob Bettson, *United Church Observer*

"He has a gift for writing. And he packs a punch."
-P. Wallace Platt, President,
St. Joseph's College, University of Alberta

The Emerging Generation, 1985

"Openly sympathetic to the aspirations and turmoils of the child-adult hybrid."
-Maclean's

"Its key findings totally smash conventional stereotypes of youth today."
-Toronto Star

Fragmented Gods, 1987

"Without a doubt, the most important book ever written on religion in Canada." -Leslie K. Tarr, Toronto journalist

"It has the unusual characteristic of being able to appeal to religious leaders, social scientists and informed people alike." -Frank S. Jones, Statistics Canada

"He tells us more about religion in Canada than we really want to know."
-Frances Ryan, *Compass*

"In the best traditions of sociology and journalism. He has woven a mass of data into a coherent and meaningful whole." -George Gallup Jr.

Mosaic Madness , 1990

"Bibby forces us to rethink our image as a nation." -Carol Goar,
Toronto Star syndicated columnist

"Just a terrific book – everyone should know about it."
-Andy Barrie, CFRB, Toronto

"A silly book." -source discarded

"Bibby argues eloquently that we must transcend our individualism and our pluralism. It should be required reading for the nation."
-Michael Valpy, *Globe and Mail*

Teen Trends, 1992

"This book is packed with information laid out in easy-to-understand tables and explained in accessible prose." *-Quill & Quire*

"An important, worthwhile work . . . with sections that can most graciously be described as sociological psycho-babble." *-Anglican Journal*

"There is much that is important, and it's presented in a direct and readable style. It's a must read for Canadian educators." *-Canadian Principal*

Unknown Gods, 1993

"Both his scholarly data and his passion make this book deserving of even more attention from the churches than that received by his landmark *Fragmented Gods*." -Robert Burkinshaw, Trinity Western University

"It's not the job of churches to sell religion like soap."
-Robert Smith, former moderator, United Church of Canada

"There is no better analysis of the current situation in Canada. A must read for every cleric in the country." -Gordon Legge, *Calgary Herald*

THE BIBBY REPORT

SOCIAL
TRENDS
CANADIAN
STYLE

REGINALD W. BIBBY

Copyright © 1995 by Reginald W. Bibby

Published in 1995 by
Stoddart Publishing Co. Limited
34 Lesmill Road
Toronto, Canada
M3B 2T6
Tel. (416) 445-3333
Fax (416) 445-5967

Stoddart Books are available for bulk purchase for sales promotions, premiums, fundraising, and seminars. For details, contact the **Special Sales Department** at the above address.

Canadian Cataloguing in Publication Data

Bibby, Reginald W. (Reginald Wayne), 1943-
The Bibby report : social trends Canadian-style

ISBN 0-7737-5748-1

1. Social surveys – Canada.   2. Canada – Social conditions –1971-   .*   I. Title.

HN103.5.B5 1995   306.6'0971   C95-931186-6

Cover Design: Angel Guerra
Printed and bound in Canada

Stoddart Publishing gratefully acknowledges the support of the Canada Council, the Ontario Ministry of Citizenship, Culture and Recreation, Ontario Arts Council, and Ontario Publishing Centre in the development of writing and publishing in Canada.

To "The Other Three"

I   -   So creative, who was taken too soon.
II   -   Who added heart and humour to the mix.
IV   -   Who has it all, and gave his all to this.

Contents

Introduction

One of my favourite sociologists, Peter Berger, once reminded readers that **we constantly are reinterpreting our biographies in the light of what is happening to us now**.[1] I'm no different.

Background

Way back in the spring of 1976, Tom Harpur of *The Toronto Star* released the findings of a national survey that I had just completed. He referred to the material as *The Bibby Report*. The media interest that followed was both startling and more than a shade overwhelming. It was flattering to be pursued by journalists and be asked to appear on programs such *Canada AM*, *As It Happens*, and the *CBC National News*. But, frankly, it was traumatic to have to face "celebs" like Norm Perry and Barbara Frum. The media stress, I assumed, would pass with the survey.

It didn't work out that way. Which takes me back to Berger. Now in 1995 I'm looking back at subsequent surveys I carried out in 1980, 1985, 1990, and this year (completed in August). I had seen that initial 1975 survey as a one-shot deal – an effort to gather fairly comprehensive information on life in Canada, focusing on social issues, intergroup relations, and religion and values. But in 1980 I thought it would be interesting to pursue the 1975 participants and see how much they had changed over the five-year period. That "ongoing core" was supplemented with new people to create a full national sample. The same procedures were repeated in 1985, 1990, and 1995. Along the way, the opportunity arose to carry out complementary national surveys of youth, and two were completed in 1984 and 1992.

Over time, I have redefined that one-shot project as an ongoing effort to monitor social trends in Canada. And I have consciously continued to work extensively with the media to make the findings available to a wide Canadian audience.

The Legacy of the 60s

It hasn't been a bad time to be lookimg at where we have come from and where we seem to be going. As every reader is well aware, the second half of this century has been a time of aggressive nation-building in Canada.

Sparked by the vigorous 60s and the leadership of Pierre Elliott Trudeau, we have been rethinking and reworking life as it is lived in this country. We've been reassessing our culture and our institutions, with a view to creating the kind of life where access to optimum living is equally possible for everyone.

Along with the United States and, increasingly, much of the rest of the world, we Canadians have been giving considerable attention to themes such as freedom and equality, tolerance and compassion, personal fulfillment and social well-being.

We've been doing more than offering rhetoric.

Ideals have been backed up with serious efforts at implementation. Major initiatives at the national level have included *The Royal Commission on Bilingualism and Biculturalism* (1963-70), *The Royal Commission on the Status of Women* (1967-70), the adoption of bilingualism and multiculturalism, the inclusion of the Charter of Rights and Freedoms as part of our first Constituion (1982), the establishment of national and provincial human rights commissions, and additional Royal Commissions addressing such concerns as human reproduction, violence against women, and aboriginal issues. Those kinds of federal efforts have been supplemented by provincial and local policies and programs aimed at enhancing life for all Canadians.

Beyond the political arena, the second half of this century has been characterized by significant demographic, social, and technological change.

- A short-list might include urbanization and urban growth; increasing immigration from Third World countries; the expansion of higher education; greater participation by women in the paid work force; the dramatic growth of the service sector; changing values, mores, and family forms; and secularization.

- Technology has seemingly exploded, with television, VCRs, camcorders, compact discs, fax machines, cellular phones, and diverse multimedia options having a profound impact on how we think, live, and relate. Computers, virtually unknown in the 50s, are now in close to one in three of our homes, with dramatic implications for the access, analysis, and dissemination of information, as well as the potential to communicate with people across the country and around the world.

The Obvious Question

So, how have we been doing?

In the face of considerable conjecture about things being "better," "worse," or "no different" as we close out the 90s, I want to take a careful look at what Canadians have been telling us about what life for them has been like in this country over the past twenty years, giving special attention to where we are today and where we seem to be headed. The surveys don't provide all the answers – I can't do it all – but they do provide many.

- The surveys have been unusually comprehensive, looking at a wide range of attitudes, beliefs, values, perceptions, and behaviour. Old themes have been tracked and new ones explored. We have exceptionally good material to work with.

- We also have access to some special people. Each sample has consisted of about 1,500 participants who have been highly representative of the Canadian population (see the appendix). But the 1995 sample of 1,800 people also includes a core of some 400 individuals who participated in *both* 1975 and 1995.

These people, *The Project Canada Panel*, will provide us with a unique glimpse of what has happened to the outlooks and behaviour of "Baby Boomers" and "Boomers' Parents" as they aged between 1975 and 1995.

• Further, through the courtesy and generosity of the Gallup organization in Canada, I occasionally will contrast some of the 1995 results with some old poll findings dating back as far as the early 40s, resulting in some treasured "longer looks."

In short, thanks primarily to some 6,000 Canadians from Newfoundland to British Columbia who participated in one to five of the surveys since 1975, we're in for a treat. I again thank them so very much for their generosity and openness.

I also am most grateful to the project's sources of funding over the years, notably the Social Sciences and Humanities Research Council of Canada, the University of Lethbridge, the United Church of Canada, CBC's *Man Alive,* and the Lilly Endowment and Lilly's Craig Dykstra and James Lewis specifically.

There are so many to thank, so little space. Thanks to Reggie, Jr., who worked so hard as project manager to ensure a solid return and quality data; to colleagues like Jack Carroll, Clark Roof, Armand Mauss, Hal Weaver, Dave Roozen, Merlin Brinkerhoff, Marilyn Nefsky, Benton Johnson, Ruth Andrews, Dean Hoge, Kirk Hadaway, Penny Marler, Don Posterski, Bill Stahl, Peter Beyer, Regina Coupar, and "Dua" for their support and friendship over the years. Many thanks to "the project people" – Jim Savoy, Michèle, Dianne, Rob, Paul, Bob, Trish, Deidre, Michelle and Pol, Elaine, Dave, and Russ. And special thanks to Jo who again was patiently and supportively there. As for the book, Don Bastian of Stoddart once more guided the process with valued competence and cherished humour.

I love life. Being a Canadian, I'm slow to give Canada some of the credit. May the book shake us up, and help us to see what's good, what's not so good, and what's possible in this country.

1 - REAFFIRMING HAPPINESS
What We Want Most Out of Life

"However weary I grow of live radio every weekday,
I still drive to work through the predawn streets of
Toronto with a sense of anticipation." -Peter Gzowski

1965	Boomers entering work force. Unemployment 3%. Inflation rate 2%. Average age of marriage for men 27, women 25. Under 9,000 divorces.
1970	Boomers continue moving into work force. Some 37% of women employed. Housing costs 7% of incomes. Less than 5% of Canadians have degrees.
1975	Thousands move to Alberta and jobs. Quebec's modernization continues. Almost 188,000 immigrants received, second largest total since 1967.
1980	Unemployment 7.5%. Iinflation rate 10%. One-year mortgage hits 18%. With falling oil prices, thousands leave Alberta. Economic mood tense.
1985	Paris-based organization rates our standard of living second only to U.S. Average age of marriage for men is 30, for women 27.
1990	Just over 10% have university degrees. More than 78,000 divorces. Federal report says Canada Pension Plan will be exhausted by 2012.
1995	Geneva group rates Vancouver 2nd, Toronto 4th, Calgary 12th in world. Unemp 11%, inflation 2%; housing 25% of incomes. Women emp: 55%.

Our Top Priorities

The surveys document what we all know well: **there is nothing that Canadians say they value more than happiness.** The trick, of course, is how to find it.

A close second "want"is **freedom.** We seem to have the notion that happiness and freedom virtually go hand-in-hand. **Most of us want the freedom to be able to do the things we want to do without having to be inhibited by people, lack of money, or lack of time.** If we are going to encounter barriers, we want the freedom to choose who or what they are going to be.

So do our children. Our 1984 and 1992 national surveys of the country's teenagers have found that they too value happiness and freedom above everything else.[1]

Other Wants

Most of us have pretty clear ideas about how we think we can find happiness – and presumably freedom as well.

• We look first and foremost to **relationships** in the form of family life and friendship, and admit we want to **be loved.**

• Yet, while we want people, our desire for freedom means that we also crave **privacy**.

• We assume happiness and freedom will be realized as we experience **success** and the accompanying financial rewards that make for physical **comfort.**

TOP 10 WANTS *"Very Important"*	
1. Happiness	89%
2. Freedom	87
3. Family life	86
4. Being loved	82
5. Friendship	77
6. Privacy	77
7. A comfortable Life	66
8. Success	60
9. A rewarding career	53
10. Keeping fit	41

• And, given how much of our lives we give to our means of "making a living," many of us give a lot of importance to having **rewarding careers.** For some people, though, that's something of a bonus, secondary to knowing success and its comforts.

• I've treated **good health** as a given; without it, not much of this matters; **keeping fit** specifically is highly valued by 4 in 10.

• Some areas of life that are important to about 30 to 35% of people include **spirituality, religion,** and **recognition.** Most of us, incidentally, aren't all that big on **excitement** (25%), **especially as we get older.**

In Canada, we make much of our diversity. Yet, when it comes to what we want out of life, we have a great deal in common. Differences by region, gender, and age, for example, are very small.

Some Key Wants by Region, Gender, and Age: 1995
"Very Important"

	Freedom	Family	Privacy	Comfort	Career
Nationally	**87%**	**86**	**77**	**66**	**53**
BC	93	77	76	67	47
Prairies	90	93	77	64	44
Ontario	87	90	79	71	53
Quebec	85	79	74	57	60
Atlantic	84	87	76	75	57
Women	87	89	80	66	54
Men	88	84	74	67	51
18-34	88	85	78	69	59
35-54	88	85	75	65	52
55+	88	88	78	65	45

• People in *B.C.* and *Quebec* are not quite as likely as others to place a high value on family life; those in Quebec are somewhat more likely to downplay comfort, yet value career.

• No noteworthy differences exist by either gender or age.

3

Some observers have been inclined to think that women who value careers do so at the expense of valuing family life. It's not the case. If anything, women in the 90s are somewhat more likely than men to place a very high value on *both* family *and* a rewarding career. **Both are coveted.**

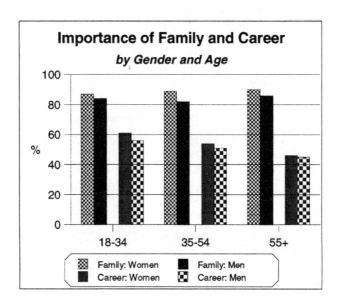

So How Are We Doing?

In the second half of this century, the goals of enhanced living and freedom have been fairly vigorously pursued in Canada.

• Since the 1960s, our *political leaders* have led the way in trying to implement policies and programs that will elevate the quality of our lives – and presumably the happiness and freedom of more and more Canadians. When they haven't, we've been quick to prod them and just about as quick to replace them.

• *Technology* has made life easier and information more accessible, while *medical advances* have made life longer and, for some, perhaps a little better.

• *Entertainment industries,* including pro sports, have been burgeoning in response to our desire to enjoy our leisure time.

It all *should* be adding up to an increase in our collective well-being. But is it?

The surveys show that since the 1970s, close to 9 in 10 Canadians have been reporting that, generally speaking, they are either *"very happy"* or *"pretty happy."* Only about 1 in 10 people have been saying they are *"not too happy."* What's more, most of us also have been inclined to view ourselves as getting happier as time goes by.[2]

Happiness and Satisfaction: 1975 Through 1995

	1975	1980	1985	1990	1995
Overall Happiness	87%	88	92	91	92
Happiness Same or Greater	**	88	87	83	82
Marital Happiness	92	93	93	92	94

People across the country also have been inclined to describe their marriages – in about 9 in 10 cases – as being either "very happy" or "pretty happy." That's been taking place, of course, at a time when a growing number of marriages have been ending in divorce.

All right, so where are all those divorces coming from?

• The downside of 90% of people claiming that their marriages are good (if not perfect) is that at any point in time, about 1 in 10 marriages are not all that great. Over their lifetimes, about 15% of Canadians are now getting divorced.

"Ever-Divorced" Canadians	
1975	7%
1980	8
1985	12
1990	14
1995	14

• What's happening is not so much that people are "fibbing" about the extent of their marital bliss. It's just that, for some, that bliss doesn't always last forever.

THE LONGER LOOK

* Happiness levels – generally and maritally – have remained steady since 1975, at about 90% and 93% respectively.

* In 1960, Gallup found that 95% of Canadians described themselves as happy, with no less than 98% reporting that they were happily married. In the process, we outdistanced nine other countries, including the U.S. Those were the alleged "happy days."

The vast majority of Canadians are happy about life.

But growing numbers are not particularly happy with what has been happening to them financially since the 1970s.

• Most people – about 75% – have been maintaining that their incomes are probably at least on a par with *other Canadians*.

• But those who are *satisfied* with their financial situation have dropped from about 85% to 70% between 1975 and 1995.

• There has been an even greater decline in the proportion of people who say that their dollar situation has either *improved* or stayed roughly the same "during the last few years" – from around 90% in 1975 to 70% in the mid-90s.

Financial Satisfaction: 1975 Through 1995

	1975	1980	1985	1990	1995
Financially Satisfied	84%	85	74	70	72
Income Average or Better	**	79	76	76	75
Financial Trend Same/Better	89	81	80	75	70
Life Avg Person Getting Worse	46	54	51	69	70

In light of growing concern about the deterioration of personal finances, it's noteworthy that **there has been a large increase in the perception that "the lot of the average person" is getting worse** – from some 45% in 1975 to 70% at present.

PROJECT CANADA FAST-FACTS
Some 64% of Canadians say that they tend to have less "extra money" on hand than they had in 1990, 21% say things are about the same, and just 15% report that they seem to have more extra dollars.

Who's Feeling What

Happiness with life as a whole is fairly constant at about 90% across the country; the same is true of *marital happiness*.

While there's little variation in *financial satisfaction*, the sense that one's *financial situation* is staying the same or improving is highest in B.C. and lowest in Quebec.

Happiness and Satisfaction Across the Country: 1995

	NAT	BC	PR	ON	QUE	ATL
Overall Happiness: High	92%	90	91	93	91	93
Marital Happiness: High	93	96	94	95	90	95
Financial Satisfaction	72	74	75	71	69	72
Financial Trends	70	81	66	69	66	72

Despite the overall level of satisfaction that we ourselves have with life, many of us still seem to have a sense that life as a whole has been getting worse in the past few decades for "the average person."

Perhaps such perception reflects reality, maybe our exposure to the problems of others via the media. Either way, it's a view has become increasingly prevalent everywhere since the mid-70s, particularly so in Quebec and the four Atlantic provinces.

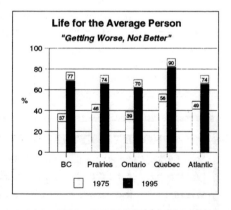

Considerable effort has been made in the post-1960s to enhance the lives of women and cultural minorities.

With respect to **gender,** the surveys show that:

• a growing majority of women have been reporting high levels of happiness, but their level of marital happiness continues to be marginally below that reported by men;

• women and men are both reporting similar levels of declining financial satisfaction since 1975.

Happiness and Satisfaction, Women and Men 1975 Through 1995		1975	1985	1995
HAPPY	Women	84%	90	94
	Men	91	94	90
HAPPILY	Women	87	89	90
MARRIED	Men	96	95	96
FINANCIALLY	Women	81	71	71
SATISFIED	Men	87	77	72
FINANCIALLY	Women	86	78	69
SAME/BETTER	Men	92	82	70
LIFE WORSE	Women	56	52	79
AVG PERSON	Men	52	50	76

As for **cultural background and race:**

• there have been only minor differences in the levels of happiness and financial satisfaction reported by people of British, French, and other national backgrounds – except for finances in 1995, where "others" are somewhat less satisfied;

• whites, until recently, have been somewhat more inclined than others to indicate that they are both happy and satisfied financially; however, as of the mid-90s, the differences are negligible – in sharp contrast to pronounced racial differences in the mid-80s, especially financially.

Happiness and Satisfaction by Cultural Group and Race 1975 Through 1995

		1975	1985	1995
HAPPY	British	87	92	94
	French	91	91	92
	Other	83	95	88
	Whites	88	92	92
	Others	82	82	91
FINANCIALLY	British	83	74	74
SATISFIED	French	87	76	73
	Other	84	71	65
	Whites	84	74	72
	Others	74	51	70

There has been considerable speculation about changing economic conditions and "Baby Boomers" – people born between approximately 1945 and 1965, who are now about 30 to 50 – along with their children, the infamous "20-somethings," who are also known as "Generation X."[3]

Boomers are seen as a generation that benefitted considerably from the best years of Canada's movement into the modern post-industrial period, knowing sizable educational, occupational, and income gains over the parents.

Their children, however, are viewed as not being able to experience similar gains. In fact, young adults under about 35 supposedly have a comparatively bleak future. Many are said to lack hope and presumably are not all that enthralled with life.

The findings lend limited support to such arguments.

• Boomers and their children exhibit similar levels of happiness as their parents and grandparents.

• Financial satisfaction levels are down for boomers' kids, but they also are down for both boomers and boomers' parents.

Intergenerational Happiness and Financial Satisfaction 1975 and 1995

	1975	1995
OVERALL HAPPINESS		
Boomers' Grandparents	87%	**
Boomers' Parents	86	92
Boomers	89	90
Boomers' Kids	**	94
FINANCIAL SATISFACTION		
Boomers' Grandparents	83	**
Boomers' Parents	88	81
Boomers	81	69
Boomers' Kids	**	67

In short, Generation X as a whole is expressing about the same level of happiness as at least the three generations before them, including their boomer parents when they were their age.

Financially, it's true 20-somethings are indicating less satisfaction than their parents were two decades ago. But, reflecting the Canadian economy as a whole in recent years, Boomers and Boomers' Parents also are less satisfied than they were in 1975. Dollar concerns are real, just not unique to Boomers' Kids.

TREND TRACKING

When it comes to wants, Canadians have been demonstrating striking uniformity. We want, above everything else, to experience happiness and freedom, and turn primarily to relationships and financial resources to attain both. Most of us are saying that we are pretty happy with life overall. However, growing numbers are expressing dissatisfaction with what is happening to them financially. If we are older, many have anxiety about whether we will be able to sustain the level of living we have known. If we are younger, we are not at all sure that we are going to be able to stay relatively close to the life standard many of us have known growing up.

That seems to be our current paradox – happy but concerned. We're not quite sure how all of this is going to turn out.

THE PROJECT CANADA PANEL

	NO CHANGE	HIGHER	LOWER	TOTALS
Overall Happiness				
Baby Boomers	71%	11	18	100
Boomers' Parents	69	19	12	100
Financial Satisfaction				
Baby Boomers	54	14	32	100
Boomers' Parents	55	16	29	100

In this and other **PROJECT CANADA PANEL** reports, we are looking at the close to 400 people who participated in both 1975 and 1995 and literally comparing them with themselves — what they said when asked the same questions twenty years apart.

2 - RETHINKING ENJOYMENT
Our Greatest Likes and Loves

*"I think that's what saved me for many
years, this capacity to blot everything
out by doing something else."
-René Lévesque*

1965	*The Tommy Hunter Show* is launched; under 10% have colour television.. *Sound of Music* wins the Academy Award for best picture.
1970	Montreal beats Calgary 23-10 in Grey Cup. Vancouver enters NHL. *Laugh-in* North America's most-watched TV program. Beatles break up.
1975	Cable TV, rare in 1970, is now found in 40% of Canadian homes. Montreal preparing for 1976 Olympics, Blue Jays for 1976 debut.
1980	Oscar Peterson wins Grammy. Gaetan Boucher wins silver. Lennon killed. Oilers, Jets, and Nords end first NHL season; Atlanta moves to Calgary.
1985	Margaret Atwood's *The Handmaid's Tale* wins Gov-General's award. Lemieux NHL's top rookie. Coke revives Classic. Toronto to build dome.
1990	*Dances With Wolves* wins Academy Award for best picture. Oilers best Boston 4-1, fifth Cup in seven years; Ottawa admitted to NHL
1995	Vancouver, Toronto join NBA. Villeneuve wins Indy 500. Nordiques move to Denver. CFL moves into 3 US cities. Carol Shields wins Pullitzer.

In our quest for the good life, complete with happiness and freedom, we engage in a wide variety of activities with people who matter to us.

During the second half of this century, technological advances, accelerated consumption, Americanization, and globalization have combined to dramatically increase both the range of those activities and the choices that are available. We have the opportunity to do more things in far more ways – whether we're talking anything from TV to travel, or from software to sex.

What We Enjoy Most

Reflecting our greatest wants, there is nothing we say we enjoy more than family life and friends. More specifically, marriage and other significant relationships, children, brothers and sisters, and parents (almost 75% for those who have them) are the major sources of enjoyment for most Canadians.

Closely behind family and friends are the places we call home – our houses and apartments – and music. Those two features provide a context for good relationships. And they also are enjoyed in private.

• About 70% of us also get a lot of enjoyment from our **cities and communities.**

• **Television** is typically watched frequently but passively: it's cited as a major source of enjoyment by 60%.

• **Jobs** are not just not a means to an end but a key source of enjoyment for more than 1 in 2 people, including about 75% who are employed full-time.

• About 50% say they get high levels of enjoyment from **sports,** about the same number as say their lives are a bit happier because of those less publicized but more reliable and lovable surrogate family members – **pets.**

TOP 10
Sources of Enjoyment
"Great Deal" or "Quite a Bit"

1. Family life	93%
2. Friends	93
3. House or apartment	82
4. Music	85
5. Marriage/relationship	76
6. City/town live in	68
7. Children	67
8. Siblings	63
9. Television	60
10. Job	56

Some Significant Others

Parents	50
Sports	50
Pets	46
Household work	35
Religious group	28

• **Household work** is something that about 35% of Canadians view as associated with high enjoyment.

• Just over 1 in 4 say they receive considerable enjoyment from their **religious group** – approximately the same proportion as are highly involved.

What we say we are doing is fairly consistent with what we say we enjoy. On a weekly basis:

• about 90% of us are trying to follow what's going on around us, while taking some time for ourselves – mainly through *music* and *reflection* – and also for our *families*;

• each week about 80% of Canadians are watching some *TV*, yet trying to get some *exercise*; we also are spending time with *friends*;

• about 60% of us are engaged in a wide array of activities, including *eating out* and *reading, hobbies*, and watching *videos;*

• about half of us do such diverse things as engage in *sex*, follow *sports*, buy *lottery tickets*, and *pray;*

• 1 in 2 use *computers*, 18% *the Internet/E-mail.*

TOP 20 ACTIVITIES Do Weekly or More*	
1. Keep up with the news	96%
2. Listen to music	93
3. Read the newspaper	89
4 Sit and think	89
5. Spend time with family	84
6. Watch TV	78
7. Exercise	71
8. Spend time with friends	71
9. Read magazines	61
10. Eat out	60
11. Read books	59
13. Engage in a hobby	55
14. Videos at home*	55
19. Go out relaxing meal*	53
16. Follow sports	53
18. Use a computer	51
15. Buy a lottery ticket*	51
17. Pray privately	48
20. Play a sport*	41

*2-3 times a month or more.

Some other activities that involve "going out" are also important sources of enjoyment, but would be expected to be done a little less often than most "the top 20" activities.

• Approximately 3 in 10 Canadians indicate that they go out to a *lounge* or *bar* or go *dancing* at least once a month, while the same number report that they catch a *movie* or a *sports event* that often.

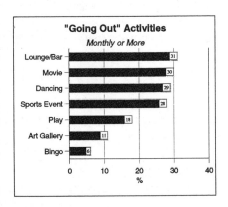

"Going Out" Activities
Monthly or More

Activity	%
Lounge/Bar	31
Movie	30
Dancing	29
Sports Event	28
Play	18
Art Gallery	11
Bingo	6

• Two in 10 say they go to a *play* about once a month, while around 1 in 10 visit an *art gallery*.

• About 1 in 20 people play *bingo* once a month or more.

Differences Between Women and Men

Perhaps surprisingly, in 1980, there were relatively few differences in how women and men were spending their time.

• Women were only slightly more likely than men to claim that they were spending time with their *families* – although, of course, the actual amount of time spent with children, for example, in a given day was undoubtedly greater. Women also were more likely than men to be reading *books* and *magazines*.

• For their part, the main activity area that differentiated men from women was *sports*: more men than women were following sports, attending sports events, and playing sports.

As of 1995, those few gender differences have diminished somewhat.

• Slightly more women than men continue to spend time with their families, and read books.

• Marginally more women are also now following sports and attending sports events; there also has been a significant increase in the proportion of women who are participating in some kind of sporting activity.

17

Select Activities of Women and Men: 1980 and 1995

	1980		1995	
	Women	Men	Women	Men
VERY OFTEN*				
Spend time with family	79%	73	68	75
Watch TV more than 5 hours	73	75	75	80
Read the newspaper	68	72	69	76
Read books	64	43	60	41
Follow sports	17	42	29	52
Play a sport	11	18	11	19
SOMETIMES				
Go to a movie	76	76	88	89
Dance	74	76	76	76
Go to a play	66	59	75	69
Attend a sports event	58	70	75	85
Go out to a lounge or bar	51	53	60	66

The 1980 response category used here is *"Very Often"*; the 1995 response category
is *"Several Times a Week or More."* Family and following sports data is first half
of the table not available for 1980; 1985 data used.

**Overall, for both sexes, there has been a slight increase in
both TV viewing and participation sports. There also has
been a modest increase in engaging in "the going out"
activities – movies, plays, sports events, bars, and the like.**
Elsewhere, activity levels have remained fairly constant.

The Longer Look

In the 1995 survey, respondents were asked, "When you are choosing a
movie, which do you want to know first, who is in it, or what it's about?"
The item was a repeat of a summer 1948 Gallup item.

	Both	What	Who	Don't Go	Totals
1995	51%	30	6	13	100
1948	18	44	21	17	100

Some Reflections on Television

Since the 1970s, we've been watching a lot more television.

• About 70% of Canadians were watching TV more than five hours a day in 1975; today the five-plus figure is just over 80%.

• Whereas some 20% of us were watching more than 16 hours of programming a week in 1975, that level reached 30% by the mid-80s, and has been around 33% since 1990.

Weekly Television Viewing: 1975-1995					
	1975	**1980**	**1985**	**1990**	**1995**
5 hours or less	32%	26	23	19	19
6-15 hours	47	46	47	48	48
16-30 hours	16	23	23	24	30
More than 30 hours	5	5	7	9	3

And what are we watching?

As of the mid-90s, we're watching a lot of American TV programs via both Canadian channels and a burgeoning number of U.S. channels.

Of interest and significance, the amount of Canadian programming available appears to be greatest in Quebec, primarily because of a large number of French channels.

Content-wise, we're watching news programs more than anything else. Approximately 85% of us are regular news viewers.

• At the same time, about 55% of us enjoy lightening up with *comedies* and immersing ourselves in movies.

• Some 50% are giving frequent attention to *documentaries* and programs that we regard as *educational*.

• *Sitcoms*, along with *drama* and *music*, are of particular interest to about 40% of the overall population, and 1 in 2 women.

• *Sports* also has a viewing audience of around 40%, led by 50% of men.

• *Talk shows, soaps,* and *game shows* know markets of some 20-25%, including 40% of women.

• Coming in last are *religious programs*, frequently watched by just 9%.

TOP 10 *Most Watched Types of* *TV Programs* Viewing "Very" or "Fairly Often"	
1. News	86%
2. Comedy: general	55
3. Movies	53
4. Documentaries	53
5. Educational	50
6. Sitcoms	45
7. Music	40
8. Sports	40
9. Drama	38
10. Talk shows	26
Also-Rans...	
Soaps	22
Game shows	19
Religious programs	9
Honorable Mention	
Weather	69

With due respect to *weather* programming, there's little reason to believe that people give weather more than a quick, if careful glimpse. Still, it's undoubtedly a commentary on our unpredictable Canadian climate that 65% of us say we often catch weather programs.

The Longer Look

* Incidentally, at least we're optimistic when it comes to coping with our weather. Some 61% think our winters are getting warmer.
* In 1955, Gallup found that an even higher 70% thought the same thing.

Some Reflections on Sports

As we have seen, sports are of particular interest to Canadian men. In recent years, thanks to the arrival of major league baseball, basketball, and hockey, and the tremendous television exposure given to sports, **Canadians have been given the opportunity of sharing in "the North American sports marketplace" to an unprecedented extent. Yet, we are showing a rather remarkable tendency to continue to embrace Canadian sports.**

• "The Big Three" sports as far as television interest are the *NHL,* major league *baseball,* and – in part because of the interest of women – *figure skating.*

• The *CFL* and *NFL* know very similar levels of viewing interest, a cultural anomaly in view of the much greater exposure the NFL receives in Canada via both American and Canadian networks.

• *Golf and car racing* are watched by just about as many people as football.

Sports Watched On Television "Very Often" or "Fairly Often"			
	ALL	**Women**	**Men**
The NHL	31%	21	41
Figure skating	30	42	16
ML Baseball	26	24	27
The CFL	13	7	19
Pro golf	13	8	17
Car Racing	12	8	15
The NFL	12	5	18
Curling	9	8	9
Skiing	9	9	7
Pro tennis	7	7	7
The NBA	5	3	7
Cdn university	3	3	4
Pro wrestling	4	2	5
American college	3	<1	5

• Other sports – notably the NBA and American college sports – are of less interest to Canadian TV viewers.

There are some significant variations in interest in various sports by both gender and region of the country.

• *Hockey* and *figure skating* are the most popular everywhere.

• *Major league baseball* shares that top ranking in "Blue Jay country" – Ontario; interest in baseball in Quebec, as the Expos know well, is something of a disappointment.

• The *CFL* has its largest proportional TV following in the West, followed by Ontario; fan interest suffers in the Atlantic region and especially Quebec, places without CFL teams. *NFL* interest is greatest in Ontario; Quebec stands out as having limited interest in televised games of either the NFL or CFL.

• *Curling* interest is greatest in the West and Atlantic regions, while *tennis* on TV is somewhat more popular in Ontario and Quebec – the homes of major tournaments – than elsewhere.

• Televised *NBA* games to date have their largest proportional followings in Ontario, B.C., and the Atlantic provinces.

Some Favourite TV Sports by Region							
	NHL	Skating	MLB	CFL	NFL	Curling	Tennis	NBA
Nationally	31%	30	26	13	12	9	7	5
BC	30	24	14	20	11	9	4	7
Prairies	32	26	23	27	11	16	3	1
Ontario	33	33	34	13	17	8	9	8
Quebec	30	33	22	2	5	3	9	2
Atlantic	25	25	29	8	7	12	4	6

The professional sports to which the media more generally give primary attention are hockey, baseball, football, and basketball. For all the hype, just how interested are average Canadians? I only started to chart some specifics here in 1990, but already the findings are intriguing.

• Approximately 40% of Canadians closely follow the NHL, with 30% actively following major league baseball.

• In the case of football, the figures slip considerably, to about 15% for both the CFL and NFL.

• Despite the presence of new NBA teams in Toronto and Vancouver, in the year that the Raptors and Grizzlies make their debut, only 7% of Canadian adults say they closely follow the National Basketball Association – a modest increase from 4% in 1990. Of particular importance, NBA interest in Toronto stands at 12%, in Vancouver at 18%.

There's been little change in the interest rankings of the four sports since the turn of the decade. All leagues, except the CFL, have modestly increased their "market shares."

		NHL	BASE	CFL	NFL	NBA
Intergenerational Interest in Major Pro Sports						
Follow "Very Closely" or "Fairly Closely"						
ADULTS	1995	38	28	16	13	7
	1990	36	24	16	11	4
TEENS	1992	44	33	22	26	28

Despite the intense competition in the sports marketplace, the current popularity rankings of "the big four" sports differ only slightly from the what they were as far back as at least the early 1940s. And there may be little change in those rankings in at least the immediate future.

The Longer Look

A Gallup poll released in February of 1942 found that 59% of Canadians said their favourite sport was hockey, 17% said baseball, and just 8% said football. Basketball — despite being invented by a Canadian — wasn't cited by so much as 1% of the populace.

• The sports that Boomers' Kids are sold on? Hockey, then baseball, then football, then basketball.

Intergenerational Interest in Major Pro Sports						
		NHL	**MLB**	**CFL**	**NFL**	**NBA**
Boomers' Kids	(18-34)	47	29	18	6	6
Boomers	(35-54)	31	26	12	10	2
Boomers' Parents	(55+)	35	29	27	11	2

Boomer offspring, however, are flirting with the NFL if they are in Ontario (31% NFL vs. 16% CFL) and B.C. (38% vs. 22%). On the Prairies things are reversed (13% vs. 20%), while "Boomer's Kids" in Quebec and the Atlantic region are indifferent to both leagues. The flirtation may be passing or permanent.

Yet with teenagers, Boomers' Kids, and Boomers themselves, a pattern is evident: **in the course of being deluged with U.S. sports, Canadians haven't abandoned CFL football. Rather, they have become more interested in the NFL** *as well.*

That's why many have mixed feelings about the NFL coming to Canada. Asked in the 1995 survey about the idea, some 65% said they *"don't really care much either way"* – reflecting current football interest. Among the rest, 41% said they don't want the NFL in Canada, 31% like the idea, *"but only if*

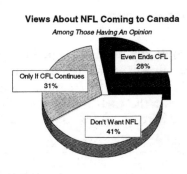

Views About NFL Coming to Canada
Among Those Having An Opinion

Even Ends CFL 28%

Only If CFL Continues 31%

Don't Want NFL 41%

the CFL continued to operate," and only 28% said they'd like to see the NFL expand to Canada, *"even if it meant the end of the CFL."* The last did not include a majority anywhere, including Toronto – the likely destiny of such a team.

In the course of pursuing happiness, freedom. and the best in life that's possible, we have been continuing to look for good relationships first and foremost. We also find enjoyment in our homes and our possessions, and in a wide range of leisure activities, among them, television and – in the male case especially – sports.

Our pursuit of "the good life" has been taking us into growing contact with the United States, adding much to our lives while, at the same time, blurring our cultural distinctiveness. The example of sports, namely hockey and Canadian football, suggests that we may be exhibiting more cultural resilience and resistance than we typically realize.

Keep an eye on this faint sign of the presence of "a latent culture" and "nascent nationalism" as we turn in the next two chapters to the kind of values we continue to view as important, and the kind of culture that we've been creating.

THE PROJECT CANADA PANEL

	NO CHANGE	HIGHER	LOWER	TOTALS
Marital Happiness				
Baby Boomers	53%	9	38	100
Boomers' Parents	73	12	15	100
Amount of TV Viewing				
Baby Boomers	26%	38	36	100
Boomers' Parents	26	60	14	100

3 - REEVALUATING VALUES
Traits We Think Are Important

"A country is something that is built every day out of certain basic shared values." -Pierre Trudeau

1965	Major programs readied for 1966 implementation. Canada Assistance Plan re: social assistance cost-sharing, Canada and Quebec Pension plans.
1970	Interim report of LeDain Commission on drugs tabled in Commons. Manitoba first province to let hockey fans buy beer without leaving seats.
1975	Bill to establish Human Rights Commission introduced in Commons. Ontario police instructed to lay charges re: violence in hockey games.
1980	Canada boycotts Moscow Olympics to protest Afghanistan invasion. Canada receives 40,000 refugees, 25,000 from Vietnam.
1985	Canada participates in world-wide *Live Aid* concert for starving Africans. Dave Stieb signs with Blue Jays for $16.6 million over seven years.
1990	Dubin report on drugs released in aftermath of Ben Johnson scandal. Canada second only to US in refugees accepted between 1975 and 1988.
1995	Report shows charitable giving $3.35 billion in 1993; up 5% from 1992. Judge rules spanking a child is no crime.

There is considerable conjecture about what is happening to values in Canada. Some see an increasing number of Canadians lacking the interpersonal values necessary for social life "to work." Others are less troubled, maintaining that values pertaining to the importance of life and good interpersonal relations are as widespread as ever.

For their part, average Canadians are skeptical. Asked to respond to the statement, *"In general, values in Canada have been changing for the worse,"* in 1985, 54% agreed.

• By 1990, the figure had reached 67%.

• As of 1995, those in agreement that values are deteriorating has reached 74%.

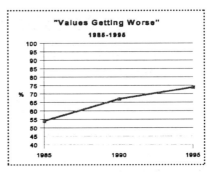

The post-1950s have been characterized by an increasing emphasis on the individual and the idea that truth is relative. In the 90s, we are seeing the results.

• Asked in 1990 to respond to the statement, *"Everything's relative,"* 65% of Canadians agreed. As of 1995, the figure has risen to 73%.

• In 1990, people were also to respond to the statement, *"What's right or wrong is a matter of personal opinion."* No less than 50% agreed. The 1995 figure? A similar 50%.

• Incidentally, among teens, as of 1992, the agreement level for the same "personal opinion" item was an even higher 65%.[1]

On the surface at least, when such large numbers of people believe that "truth is up for grabs," it's difficult to get consensus on values. For example, if a person were to suggest that there is a need for instilling "better values" in young people, the reflexive reaction in Canada would be to say, "Whose values?"

Since 1985, I have been attempting to get an idea of what kinds of interpersonal traits are important to Canadians. I've had two questions in mind. First, I've wanted to see to what extent consensus exists on values. Second, I've wanted to explore whether or not increasing public concern about alleged value changes is, in fact, warranted.

Value Consensus

As of the mid-90s, it's apparent that considerable agreement exists on some basic interpersonal values.

• **Honesty** is highly valued by 9 in 10 Canadians.

• **Reliability and kindness** are viewed as "very important" by 8 in 10.

• About 7 in 10 people say they highly value **friendliness, concern for others**, and **politeness**.

• Just under 6 in 10 regard **forgiveness** and **generosity** as very important.

Interpersonal Values 1985 Through 1995 Seen as "Very Important"			
	1995	1990	1985
Honesty	89%	89	96
Reliability	82	81	88
Kindness	79	75	**
Friendliness	70	70	**
Concern others	68	63	**
Politeness	67	62	70
Forgiveness	57	55	75
Generosity	57	52	**

As for value shifts, **there has been a slight drop over the last decade in the proportion of Canadians placing a high value on honesty, reliability, and politeness.** Yet, for all the consternation about values possibly "changing for the worst," these and other key interpersonal traits continue to be endorsed by a fairly large majority of the population.

The most pronounced decline has been for *forgiveness* – in part the result, I suspect, of our placing premier emphasis on themes like zero tolerance. We haven't left a lot of room for error.

PROJECT CANADA FAST-FACTS

Interpersonally and otherwise, we appreciate a good laugh: in the 1995 survey, 68% of Canadians said that humour is "very important to them."

There are some variations in the valuing of these character-istics, as can be illustrated with honesty, kindness, polite-ness, forgiveness, and generosity.

• **Regionally**, these civility traits tend to be valued somewhat more highly on the Prairies and in the Atlantic region.

• Viewed by **community size**, they are only slightly less important to people in larger cities than to residents elsewhere.

Select Values by Region and Community Size
View as "Very Important"

	Honesty	Kindness	Politeness	Forgiveness	Generosity
BC	89%	82	66	58	50
Prairies	93	89	68	74	62
Ontario	88	76	66	61	53
Quebec	86	74	68	35	61
Atlantic	91	83	75	69	67
100,000+	88	77	67	55	54
90-10,000	90	82	68	61	61
<10,000	90	81	68	60	61

Gender-wise, women "bury" men in tending to be far more inclined to see all of these interpersonal traits as "very impor-tant." The differences are large and consistent, regardless of *age*. Women, whether they are Boomers' Kids, Boomers, or Boomers' Parents, place more value on all of these interpersonal traits than their male age cohort counterparts.

• A bit disconcerting is that women under the age of 35 are not quite likely as older women to endorse these civility traits.

Select Interpersonal Values by Gender and Age

	Honesty	Kindness	Politeness	Forgiveness	Generosity
Women	**91%**	**85**	**74**	**66**	**65**
18-34	86	81	68	61	59
35-54	93	88	76	71	72
55+	96	89	78	67	64
Men	**86**	**73**	**61**	**49**	**49**
18-34	80	74	61	37	45
35-54	88	70	59	53	51
55+	91	76	67	58	53

• Further, while men who are Boomers and Boomers' Parents differ little in the value they place on these characteristics, Boomers' Kids – men under the age of 35 – are far less likely than other men to see them as very important." **In short, a value shift is taking place. But it lies primarily with young adults under 35, and particularly with young men.**

Us and Them

As we have seen, many people think that values are getting worse in Canada. Yet, if we hold such a view, presumably our concern is not with us – it's with other people.

The 1995 survey checked out such a pattern. In addition to being asked about *their values*, respondents also were asked for their perception of the importance that *"Canadians in general"* give to a number of those same values.

What the survey found is that we typically think traits such as generosity, concern for others, honesty, and being loved are valued more highly by us than by people in general.

Such findings underline the fact that we Canadians have far more in common with one another than we realize. We've just been remarkably slow to grasp it.

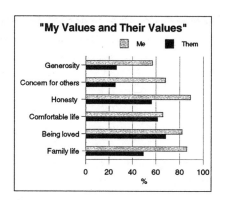

"My Values and Their Values"

Me   Them

Generosity
Concern for others
Honesty
Comfortable life
Being loved
Family life

0   20   40   60   80   100
%

PROJECT CANADA FAST-FACTS

As of 1995, 28% of Canadians feel that "the need for common values" is a "very serious" problem in the country - rating it at about the same level as the lack of unity, school violence, and drug abuse. Significantly, this is not just a concern of older people: adults of all ages are equally likely to see the need for values as a severe problem.

The Value of Contributions

One way of getting a sense of a society's values is by seeing what kind of worth we assign to the roles that people play.

In the 1995 survey, respondents were given a list of occupations and asked if people in these positions are being paid *"about the right amount of money, too much, or too little money."*

• About 85% of Canadians say that *nurses* are being paid either the right amount or too little, while some 70% say the same about *teachers* and *social workers*.

• The incomes of *mechanics and physicians* are seen as appropriate by around 60%.

Appropriate Rewards for Appropriate Contributions
"People in these occupations are being paid . . ."

	The Right Amount	Too Little	Too Much	Have No Idea	Totals
Nurses	46%	41	8	5	100
Teachers	52	21	23	4	100
Social Workers	38	32	12	18	100
Mechanics	52	12	25	11	100
Physicians	53	5	35	7	100
Dentists	37	1	57	5	100
Politicians	25	3	68	4	100
Lawyers	21	1	73	5	100
Pro Athletes	8	2	85	5	100
Average Canadians	**31**	**59**	**2**	**8**	**100**

• What *dentists* make is approved of by some 40%.

• In contrast, 73% feel that *lawyers* are being paid "too much," and 68% hold the same opinion of politicians.

• The lowest level of salary approval is shown *professional athletes*: 85% of Canadians say their salaries are excessive.

The Longer Look

Lawyers, in particular, have not been able to shed the perception that they have an inordinate interest in money. In late 1950, Gallup found that 80% of Canadians felt lawyers were too interested in making money, versus "living up to the best standards of their calling." Some 53% said the same thing of physicians, 52% of dentists.

Social Compassion

Leaders have liked to refer to Canadians as "a compassion-ate people." Yet, in the face of financial struggles and cuts to social programs in recent years, some observers have been maintaining that Canada has been losing much of its heart.

As we have just seen, large numbers of Canadians continue to place a high value on kindness and concern for others.

Despite threats to social programs, an overwhelming majority of people have continued to maintain that under-privileged Canadians have a right to an adequate income and medical care.

• True, occasional caution is expressed by some who want people to do what they can to produce income. But the general principle of providing *adequate monies* for people who are poor has been – and continues to be – solidly endorsed.

• In the case of *medical care*, Canadians are virtually unani-mous in agreeing that, when physical problems exist that require attention, those needs have to be attended to regardless of the ability of the people involved to pay.

Social Compassion: 1975 Through 1995					
	1975	1980	1985	1990	1995
People who are poor have a right to an income adequate to live on	87%	88	92	91	84
People who cannot afford it have a right to medical care	94	93	93	92	96

TREND TRACKING

Officially we Canadians seem to have an increasingly pluralistic view of our values. In actual practice, we are far less relativistic.

A growing number of people – now some 75% of the population – feel that values are deteriorating. Further, despite some slippage in the past decade, considerable consensus exists concerning the importance of many interpersonal traits, and even the importance of various occupations. Yet, we frequently think that other people don't hold the same values and views that we do.

These findings, along with those concerning what we want out of life, suggest that we have far more in common with each other than we realize. The theme of Canadian diversity has camouflaged the reality of Canadian commonalities.

All of this brings us to an important question: what does our much-heralded mosaic really mean? We'll address it next.

THE PROJECT CANADA PANEL			
	NO CHANGE	NOW AGREE	NOW DISAGREE	TOTALS
People have a right to an adequate income			
Baby Boomers	83%	4	13	100
Boomers' Parents	83	4	13	100
Traditional morality will increase by 2000			
Baby Boomers	65	20	15	100
Boomers' Parents	72	12	16	100

4 - RECREATING CULTURE
What the Mosaic Really Means

*"We have built a country that has not
simply acknowledged its own diversity
but thrived on it." -Brian Mulroney*

1965	Canadian national flag adopted following controversy. Preparations continue for centennial world's fair in Montreal in 1967.
1970	Government urges move to metric system. CRTC mandates Can content. Ryerson, oldest Can publisher, sold to U.S. group. Postal codes in 1971.
1975	CN Tower finished. Sophia Rayburn dies, 108; 4 days younger than Can. End coming for foreign-owned periodical tax breaks, incl *Time, RDigest*.
1980	*O Canada!* adopted as national anthem. Flag ceremony at Grey Cup in Toronto gets five-minute ovation. Terry Fox named to Order of Canada.
1985	Royal Canadian Mint announces new coin will replace one-dollar bill. Foster Hewitt dies. Bryan Adams wins three Junos.
1990	Richler wins award for *Solomon Gursky*. Oldest atlas collection damaged. Death claims Johnny Wayne, Harold Ballard, Whipper Billy Watson.
1995	*Front Page Challenge* cancelled; CBC announces 1,000 job cuts. US cable companies try to eliminate protection for Can broadcasting.

There is perhaps no single characteristic that we are inclined to point to more in describing Canadian uniqueness than the fact that we are a cultural mosaic.

• Faced with the problem of creating a society in which people of varied linguistic and cultural backgrounds can live together, we have decided as Canadians that we will convert a demographic reality into a national virtue.

• We have decreed that what is descriptively obvious should be prescriptively valued. Canada will be a multinational society, a mosaic of people from varied backgrounds who will have the freedom to live as they see fit.[1]

• **The assumption is that the pieces will come together to form a mosaic that is far more than merely the sum of its individual parts.** The end result will be a richer life for us all.

The Plan

Such culture-building has not taken place by accident. **The federal government has led the way in introducing two fundamental cultural building blocks: bilingualism and multiculturalism.**

While both policies technically have their sources in the 1960s and the Royal Commission on Bilingualism and Biculturalism, they reflect the age-old national quest for unity in the face of diversity.

• **Bilingualism represents a response to the precarious reality of two dominant national groups co-existing within Canada**. The official resolution is the declaration that the country has not one but two equal founding peoples. To be a Canadian is to be proficient in English, French, or both languages. And since 1969 and the passing of the Official Languages Act, linguistic duality has been enshrined.

• **Multiculturalism is the official response to a further Canadian reality – the existence of a large number of cultural groups besides those of British and French ancestry**. It is a pluralistic, "mosaic" solution, standing in contrast to the assimilationist "melting pot" ideal frequently associated with the U.S. The federal multicultural program was established in 1971; in 1988, the Canadian Multiculturalism Act was passed, also enshrining this second cornerstone policy.

Our Response

There has been considerable reluctance on the part of Canadians outside Quebec to accept the idea that French and English constitute Canada's two official languages.

• Through 1985, a modest increase took place in the endorsement of the two language concept – from 49% in 1975 to 57%. Small but consistent increases in support of bilingualism could be detected in all regions.

• However, in the past ten years, the situation has stagnated. The percentage of those favouring two official languages has levelled off at about 55%, while those wanting "English only" has remained fixed at around 35%.

• Across the country, including Quebec, support for bilingualism has not risen from 1980 levels, except on the Prairies, where very low levels simply have risen slightly. In the Atlantic region, support has slipped from a 1985 high.

Endorsement of Bilingualism: 1975 Through 1995					
	1975	1980	1985	1990	1995
Nationally	**49**	**57**	**53**	**51**	**55**
QUEBEC	71	82	89	82	81
OUTSIDE QUEBEC	41	45	46	43	46
British Columbia	37	43	43	38	46
Prairies	28	36	38	39	41
Ontario	47	51	49	46	50
Atlantic	45	43	51	43	36

Today, support for bilingualism struggles to improve on the levels observed in the first decade after the passing of the Official Languages Act in 1969.

What's more, analyses by *age over time* suggest that minimal headway is being made in convincing Canadians outside of Quebec that bilingualism is a policy worth supporting.

• The level of endorsement among adults under 35 is no greater today than in 1975.

• Further, support among 18 to 34-year-olds in 1975 fell as they moved into their late 30s, 40s, and early 50s.

Bilingualism Support Outside Quebec		
	1975	**1995**
18-34	52%	51
35-54	35	44
55+	34	43

Multiculturalism and the mosaic are also in trouble. After a positive start, support for the mosaic idea has been declining.

• In 1985, 56% said they preferred "the mosaic" and just 28% "the melting pot."

• Today, the mosaic's appeal has declined to 44%, while support for the melting pot has risen to 40%.

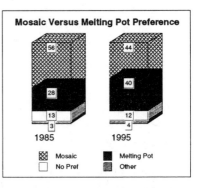

What's so striking about the shift away from the mosaic is its pervasiveness across regions, age, and educational levels.

• In both Quebec and Ontario there have been pronounced movements toward the melting pot, while people in the Prairie provinces have also been moving in that direction. Only in B.C. and the Atlantic region has there been little change; in 1995, however, B.C. led the country in embracing assimilation.

• *Age-wise*, every cohort is less inclined to opt for the mosaic than in 1985.

• The same pattern is true of *educational* groups.

Mosaic Versus Melting Pot Preferences: 1985 and 1995

| | MOSAIC | | MELTING POT | |
	1985	1995	1985	1995
BC	50%	43	38	39
Prairies	57	48	32	39
Ontario	56	46	31	44
Quebec	55	37	16	40
Atlantic	53	54	23	24
18-34	59	50	22	34
35-54	55	43	30	41
55+	51	41	33	44
Degree +	69	50	19	36
Post-Sec	50	40	29	43
HS Less	50	43	30	41

The mosaic is still preferred – bit its lead is slipping.

If we are split between preferring the mosaic and melting pot, we certainly aren't split over the idea that people coming to Canada should share in "Canadian culture."

Most Canadians expect new arrivals to do more than arrive and proceed to add a new cultural tile to the mosaic.

• In 1975, just four years after the unveiling of the multiculturalism policy, 85% of Canadians maintained that *"immigrants to Canada have an obligation to learn Canadian ways."* The 1995 figure is 88%.

• Those majorities have included some 80% of respondents who have come to Canada since the 1960s.

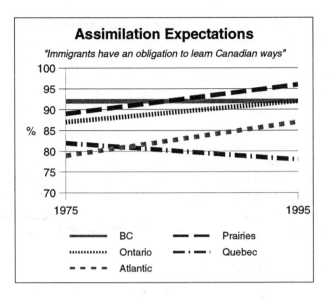

Assimilation Expectations

"Immigrants have an obligation to learn Canadian ways"

Legend:
- BC
- Ontario
- Atlantic
- Prairies
- Quebec

Our Mosaic

The game-plan was that bilingualism and multiculturalism would provide the backdrop for our cultural mosaic. Individual contributions would add up to an attractive, integrated art-piece.

One measure of our success so far might be the extent to which we have come to place a value on being Canadians – something of a "consciousness of kind."

In the first *Project Canada* survey, completed in 1975,

- 54% suggested Canadians *"are not nationalistic enough"*;
- 40% said we have *"about the right amount of nationalism"*;
- the remaining 6% said that we *"are too nationalistic."*

From the late 70s onward, at least, we've been acting like we're pretty happy to be Canadians. **There's good reason to believe we are fonder of Canada and being Canadians than most of us – including many politicians and journalists – realize.**

Despite our ongoing domestic squabbles, 9 in 10 of us – much like those married couples among us – have been saying that our being Canadian is *"very"* or *"somewhat important"* to us.

Importance of Being a Canadian 1985 Through 1995			
	1985	1990	1995
Nationally	90%	87	85
B.C.	88	91	90
Prairies	95	92	93
Ontario	93	92	92
Quebec	79	71	64
Atlantic	97	97	96

• "We" still includes just over 6 in 10 Quebeckers, but does involve a big decline from 8 in 10 only a decade ago.

• Appreciation for life in Canada is marginally higher in the Atlantic provinces than elsewhere.

PROJECT CANADA FAST-FACTS

While the 1995 survey has found that 62% of Canadians say that being a Canadian is "very important" to them, just 45% think other people also place that kind of importance on being Canadian.

Further reflecting the value placed on life in Canada, 77% of us say that, *if we could live in any country*, we would choose this one. Some 1 in 6 Quebeckers who prefer Canada specifically mention Quebec.

Preference for Living in Canada 1985 Through 1995			
	1985	1990	1995
Nationally	79%	74	80
B.C.	77	80	86
Prairies	80	74	77
Ontario	81	71	80
Quebec	76	72	78
Atlantic	84	85	89

Given the chance, 7% say we'd go to "the States," while 4% would head for Australia.

Variations that do exist in valuing Canada and wanting to live in Canada reflect differences between Quebec and the rest of Canada, rather than differences between cultural minorities and other Canadians.

• Contrary to prevalent notions, a majority of people with non-British backgrounds – including Asians and other non-Europeans – are just as likely as other people to value being Canadians and to value living in Canada.

• It's true that people from other than British countries – including those of French descent – are more inclined to value their cultural heritages. But, simultaneously, they place a high value both on being Canadians and residing in this country.

Importance of Being a Canadian, Cultural Group Heritage, and Living in Canada by Group Background

	BEING A CANADIAN	CULTURAL GROUP HERITAGE	PREFER CANADA
NATIONALLY	85%	59	80
British	92	49	81
French	65	79	67
Other European	93	61	75
Other Countries	98	60	94

Our Culture

Further to the creating of Canadian culture, most of us place a fair amount of importance on being Canadians and certainly plan to stay.

Less clear is the kind of culture that has emerged from our emphasis on tapping our multinational resources.

• Is the rest of Canada benefitting from the presence of Québécois culture? Similarly, does the presence of people from a wide array of other countries result in a new, enriched culture for everyone?

• Or, are policies like bilingualism and multiculturalism simply political panaceas with platitudinous voice-overs, with minimal impact on the culture of Canadians as a whole?

Favourites

Some clues to the nature of our emerging culture can be found by looking at the people in the culture who have an influence on us – people we draw on for our ideas and turn to for our entertainment.

In the 1995 survey, Canadians were asked about their a favourite people in the areas of news, music, sports, television, movies, books, journalism, and politics. They were instructed simply to skip spheres where no one in particular stood out.

The prevalent response was no response. Canadians seem to be light on favourites. In none of the eight areas did more than 1 in 3 of survey respondents cite a favourite.

That said, let's "open the envelopes."

• **In the areas of newscasting, politics, journalism, and sports, Canadians came in first.** Names like Robertson, Chrétien, Gzowski, and Gretzky – and in Quebec, Myriam Bédard, Jean-François Lépine, and Jean-Luc Mongrain – were among those most often mentioned.

Top Three Favourites

Newscaster	Politician	Journalist	Author
Local	Chrétien J	Lépine, J-F	King S
Robertson L	Bouchard L	Walters B	Steel D
Mansbridge P	Trudeau P	Gzowski P	Clancy T
NONE 73%	NONE 83%	NONE 86%	NONE 70%

Athlete	TV Personality	Singer	Actor/Actress
Bédard M	Winfrey O	Dion C	Hanks T
Gretzky W	Letterman D	Streisand B	Ford H
Stojko E	Mongrain, J-L	Pavarotti L	Costner K
NONE 77%	NONE 80%	NONE 66%	NONE 74%

• **But after that, the Americans and one Italian took over.** When Canadians think of authors, TV personalities, screen stars, and singers, the names that most frequently come to mind are the likes of Steel, Winfrey, Hanks, and Pavarotti. A single exception is Celine Dion, thanks primarily to a fairly heavy Quebec vote.

These findings suggest we tend to look to *Canadians* when we want *information,* and, to some extent, sports.

But when it comes to *entertainment,* our favourites are typically *American.*

And our sons and daughters are following in our footsteps. The extensive 1992 *Project Teen Canada* survey found that teens' favourites also are typically American, extending to newscasters and politicians as well![2]

Nationality of Canadian Favourites			
	Can	Amer	Other
Newscaster	88%	10	2
Politician	87	5	8
Journalist	81	11	8
Athlete	65	20	15
Singer	39	38	23
TV Personality	32	61	7
Author	25	43	32
Actor/Actress	16	71	13

There's one very important regional exception to the pattern of favourites for both teens and adults – Quebec.

• More often than elsewhere, the favourites of Quebeckers are Canadians, often from Quebec.

• The irony here is that Quebec has had grave concern since the 1950s about being overwhelmed by Anglophone culture, both Canadian and U.S.

Canadian Favourites: Quebec and the Rest of Canada		
	Quebec	Rest
Newscaster	92%	87
Athlete	90	56
Journalist	88	77
Politician	86	87
TV Personality	84	13
Singer	66	27
Author	64	12
Actor/Actress	37	8

These findings suggest that, unlike the cultural situation in the rest of Canada, Quebec's cultural preservation efforts have been highly successful.[3]

National Awareness

To the extent that Canada has been creating a national culture of some kind, people should be familiar with some of its features. Those features might include some key parts of our history, along with some of our symbols and ceremonies.

Canadians were asked a number of questions about Canada in the 1995 survey. Most came through with high marks.

• Almost no one had any difficulty with questions about the current PM, our capital, or our anthem.

• Close to 60% knew that John A. Macdonald was our first PM; almost everyone is familiar with the Stanley Cup – most also with the Grey Cup.

• Knowledge of "things American," ranging from presidents to Super Bowls, is very high.

Familiarity With Canadian and U.S. Life	
Current Prime Minister	96%
Current U.S. President	92
Canada's first PM	59
Canada's capital	95
Name of national anthem	90
Stanley Cup sport	94
Super Bowl sport	87
Grey Cup sport	81

The Longer Look

Knowledge levels about Canada today tend to exceed those of the past. Polls found in the Gallup archives show:

* In 1945, only 45% could identify "John A." as our first PM; incidentally, 88% knew that Harry Truman was the U.S. president.
* In 1950, when we had no national anthem, 48% thought it was "O Canada!"
* In 1955, just 68% knew the sport associated with the Grey Cup.

Our National Heroes

We often have been depicted as "a nation without heroes."
The concern associated with the criticism is our limited success
in developing a sense of being a people with shared experiences.

Times, both good and bad, have produced outstanding individuals who potentially can remind us of our Canadian heritage. **To
minimize our heroes is to minimize symbols that can help
bind us together.**

By way of historical perspective, Gallup explored the same issue
way back "in the summer of '42." People were asked, *"Who in
your opinion is the greatest living Canadian?"*

- Some 40% of respondents could not come up with anyone.

- Another 22% cited the Prime Minister of the day, Mackenzie
  King, while a further 15% mentioned General McNaughton.

I repeated the 1942 Gallup item in the 1995 survey, and added
a similar item: *"Who, in your opinion, is the greatest Canadian
of all time?"* In both cases, people were given an opportunity to
list someone, or to indicate that "no one comes to mind."

- Regarding *the greatest living Canadian*, the 1995 respondents outdid their 1942
counterparts in drawing
blanks: 76% either said
that "no one comes to
mind" or said nothing.

- *Pierre Trudeau* was
mentioned by 10% of
the total sample – a
good 9 points ahead of
anyone else.

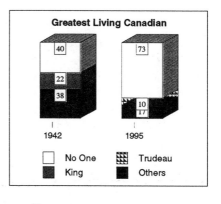

47

Given the chance to expand the time-frame considerably, and indicate who, in their opinion, is *the greatest Canadian of all time*, a stunning 58% indicated that "no one comes to mind"! Another 15% didn't offer a response.

The remaining 25% of Canadians picked Pierre Trudeau as number one, with politicians filling the second and third spots as well. Terry Fox and the medical duo of Banting and Best filled out the top five.

Top 5 Canadians of All Time

1. Pierre E. Trudeau
2. John A. Macdonald
3. Lester B. Pearson
4. Terry Fox
5. Fred. Banting and Chas. Best

Our National Inferiority Complex

The findings so far show Canadians – particularly those outside of Quebec – drawing fairly heavily on American life to supplement Canadian culture.

Could the reason we don't seem to have many heroes be that "the real heroes" are defined by the Americans – that our cultural worth and sometimes even our personal worth is defined by the U.S.?

In probing how we feel about ourselves, relative to how we feel about Americans, I repeated a procedure I had used in the 1992 *Project Teen Canada* survey. Early in the questionnaire, I gave participants five characteristics – *"risk-takers," "generous," "confident," "world's best at what they do,"* and *"patriotic"*– and asked them to estimate how well they felt the traits describe *Americans*. Later in the questionnaire, I repeated the item, this time asking respondents how well they felt the characteristics describe *Canadians*.

• Adults and teenagers hold fairly similar perceptions of both Canadians and Americans with respect to confidence, patriotism, and risk-taking – the Americans win easily.

• Adults, however, break with teenagers on one important characteristic. By a slight margin, adults maintain that the description *"world's best at what they do"* better describes Canadians than Americans.

• By quite a wide margin, adults feel that *generosity* is a trait that better characterizes Canadians than Americans.

Applicability of Traits to Canadians and Americans
Traits Describe "Very Well" or "Fairly Well"

| | ADULTS | | TEENAGERS | |
	Canadians	*Americans*	*Canadians*	*Americans*
Confident	61%	87	66%	91
Patriotic	58	92	47	89
Generous	84	53	**	**
Risk-takers	33	82	43	84
World's best	56	48	40	62

PROJECT CANADA FAST-FACTS
In the face of what appears to be a growing Americanization of Canadian life, economically and culturally, the perception that Americans have "too much power in our nation's affairs" has not increased since the 70s.
1975: 72%   1980: 61%   1985: 52%   1990: 58%   1995: 54%

TREND TRACKING

In responding to our cultural and linguistic diversity with bilingualism and multiculturalism, we hoped to experience not only unity in diversity but also enhanced living through diversity.

But in the past two decades, we have been reluctant to accept either policy. Today, despite bilingualism, we are still facing the prospect of Quebec leaving Canada. Culturally, while Quebec has succeeded in retaining distinctiveness, multiculturalism has been adding up to a cultural blank in the rest of the country. People in "the rest of Canada" have a questionable sense of where they have come from, few heroes, and a passive acceptance of being inferior to the U.S. In lieu of having our own "Canadian culture," our tendency has been to fill the void with American culture, resulting in an intensified "Americanization of Canadian life."

Still, as we will see shortly, if bilingualism and multiculturalism haven't resulted in our tapping our diversity for our collective good, the two policies have helped to make life easier and better for many Canadians.

THE PROJECT CANADA PANEL

	NO CHANGE	NOW AGREE	NOW DISAGREE	TOTALS
Favour Bilingualism				
Baby Boomers	71%	16	13	100
Boomers' Parents	70	17	13	100
Immigrants Should Learn "Canadian Ways"				
Baby Boomers	85	13	2	100
Boomers' Parents	86	10	4	100

5 - REWORKING RELATIONS
What We're Thinking About Each Other

"One of the strongest messages from citizens is their belief in equality and fairness as guiding principles for our society." -The Citizens' Forum on Canada's Future

1965	Canada receives almost 150,000 immigrants, largest number since 1957. Freedom movements peaking re: women, Natives, minorities, Quebec.
1970	Keith Spicer, 36, appointed first language commissioner. B & B Commission releases vol. 4 on "other" ethno-cultural groups.
1975	Fed govt announces summer programs to head off threats of racial tension. Committee suggests annual immigration quota, locating in smaller cities.
1980	Natives take Constitutional concerns to London and to UN. Ontario passes legislation to protect woman from sexual harassment.
1985	Jim Keegstra found guilty of willfully promoting hatred against Jews. Bill passed restoring Indian and band status to women who had lost it.
1990	RCMP announces turbans and braids can be worn by officers in uniform. Post-70s pattern of more immigration from Asian than Europe accelerates.
1995	Municipality delegates want tougher treatment of violent young offenders. Statistics Canada says crime down significantly.

A major emphasis of the Trudeau years was justice and equality. The Liberal government of the 60s and 70s wanted to create a Canada where cultural minorities and women, for example, could participate fully in Canadian life.

• Those themes have continued to be emphasized through the 80s and 90s, with Conservative and Liberal governments expanding category priorities to include Natives, gays and lesbians, along with the handicapped, abused, and exploited.

• Such a strong emphasis on justice and equality has, of course, been essential and has done much to improve life for many people. It also has had some costs.

51

Intergroup Relations

Canada is still a long way away from full cultural and racial harmony. But since the late 60s and early 70s when bilingualism and multiculturalism were officially enshrined, **in the midst of frequent charges of rising racism and growing conflict, intergroup relations have shown signs of improvement.**

Perceived Discrimination

Despite our emphasis on the acceptance of cultural diversity, some 65% of Canadians acknowledge that racial and cultural groups are being discriminated against in their communities – up from 55% in 1980.

• Since 1980, the percentage of Canadians who think discrimination *is getting worse* has averaged about 15%, while about 15% also have been reporting that a problem exists, but that *things are improving.* A further 30% have agreeing that discrimination exists, but say it is *no better or worse.*

• Among the 40% who have not been feeling that discrimination is a problem, 10% think that their communities *used to* have such problems but no longer do, while 30% say that discrimination has *never* been a problem where they live.

Perceived Discrimination: 1980 Through 1995

"Do you feel that any racial or cultural groups in your community are discriminated against?"

	YES	Worse	Better	Same	No	Prob Past	Never Prob	TOTALS
1995	67	14	20	33	33	9	24	100
1990	59	18	16	25	41	8	33	100
1985	54	9	17	28	46	10	36	100
1980	55	14	15	26	45	9	30	100

What's increased in the mid-90s in the sense that, "Yes, discrimination exists, but it's really no better or worse."

Regionally, Quebec residents are the most likely to report racial and cultural group discrimination, the Atlantic region the least.

• Nevertheless, since 1980, people in all regions except B.C. are reporting discrimination increases, with the jumps particularly high in Ontario and the Atlantic provinces.

Interestingly, there is little difference by **cultural group** in the inclination to acknowledge that discrimination exists.

		YES	Worse Now	Better Now	Same	NO	Prob Past	Never A Prob	TOT
BC	1995	**67**	23	12	32	**33**	7	26	100
	1980	**71**	21	14	36	**29**	8	21	100
Prairies	1995	**64**	11	19	34	**36**	8	28	100
	1980	**55**	14	7	34	**45**	7	38	100
Ontario	1995	**63**	13	17	33	**37**	11	26	100
	1980	**49**	16	12	21	**51**	7	44	100
Quebec	1995	**75**	15	28	32	**25**	8	17	100
	1980	**65**	12	27	26	**35**	13	22	100
Atlantic	1995	**58**	4	21	33	**42**	11	31	100
	1980	**32**	2	11	19	**68**	5	63	100

Perceived Discrimination: 1980 and 1995
"Do you feel that any racial or cultural groups in your community are discriminated against?"

PROJECT CANADA FAST-FACTS
The perception Native-White relations is a "Very Serious Problem":
1975 - 16%   1980 - 15%   1990 - 23%   1995 - 18%

Intergroup Attitudes

Beyond perception, what are we thinking and feeling?

One measure of our acceptance of one another is our receptivity to the idea of intermarriage.

There has been a gradual increase in the approval of marriages between Canadians of different cultural and religious groups since at least the 1970s.

• Particularly striking are the increases in approval for marriages of whites and Asians, along with whites and blacks.

• Still, about 15-20% of Canadians are opposed to some forms of cultural group intermarriage, and some 10% have difficulty with marriages involving Protestants, Catholics, and Jews.

Approval of Intergroup Marriage: 1975 Through 1995

	1975	1980	1985	1990	1995
Whites and Natives	75%	80	83	84	84
Whites and Asians (Orientals)	66	75	78	82	83
Whites and East Indians/Pakistanis	58	66	72	77	80
Whites and Blacks	57	64	72	79	81
Protestants and Roman Catholics	86	88	89	90	92
Protestants and Jews	80	84	84	86	90
Roman Catholics and Jews	78	81	82	85	89

As another measure of our attitudes toward various cultural groups, I have been looking at the perception we have of their power in Canadian life.

The surveys have asked respondents to indicate if they feel a number of well-known cultural groups have *"Too Much Power," "Too Little Power,"* or about the *"Right Amount of Power"* in *"our nation's affairs."* Objectively, what has characterized all of these groups is their relative lack of power. Consequently, to say that they have "too much power" is being interpreted as a negative view of a group.

• Over the past two decades a core of about 15% of Canadians have maintained that East Indians/Pakistanis, other Asians, and Jews have "too much power" in Canadian life.

• In the case particularly of Natives, along with South Pacific Asians, there has been an increase since the mid-80s in the perception that they have excessive power.

Perception Groups Have *"Too Much Power"* 1975 Through 1995

	1975	1980	1985	1990	1995
Natives	7%	6	13	18	33
East Indians/Pakistanis	**	16	15	22	18
Jews	28	13	13	13	14
Whites	**	**	**	17	9
Asians (Orientals)	**	**	7	14	16
Blacks	**	**	5	7	9

PROJECT CANADA FAST-FACTS
In the 1995 survey, respondents were asked about their views of "visible minorities" generally with respect to marriage and power.
Approve of White-Visible Minority marriages: 87%.
Feel Visible Minorities have too much power: 20%.

Regionally,

• the perception that *Natives* have "too much power"is currently highest in Quebec and the West;

• the same sentiment toward *South Pacific Asians* is most prevalent in British Columbia;

• and the idea that *blacks* have more power than they should have is highest in Ontario.

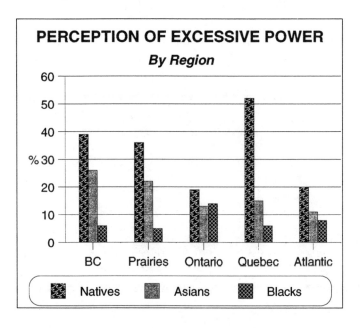

Overall, the "too much power" numbers are fairly small. Yet, they are disturbing because they indicate that pockets of bigotry continue to exist. Further, the variations over time remind us that they can readily fluctuate in response to ongoing developments. Progress is hardly inevitable.

As a third measure of intergroup relations, Canadians have been asked since 1975 what their immediate reaction is when they are in the presence of a person, and know only one thing about him or her – in this case, the person's cultural group background.

From the 70s through the 90s, the general pattern has been for a decreasing number of people to indicate that they would feel uneasy around such "visible minorities."

Feelings of Uneasiness: 1975 Through 1995

	1975	1980	1985	1990	1995
East Indians/Pakistanis	**	22%	18	16	15
Blacks	16	11	11	9	11
Asians (Orientals)	14	9	9	7	8
Natives	13	14	9	10	9
Jews	9	7	8	7	6

• On the positive side, some 90% of Canadians say that they would be comfortable in the presence of just about anyone.

• On the negative side, as with perception of excessive power, there continues to be a core of as many as 10% of Canadians who express awkwardness around almost any minority group member. And some 15% continue to express uneasiness in the presence of East Indians and Pakistanis.

Differences by **region** in part reflect the contact people have with members of various groups.

• The greatest awkwardness with Asians generally is expressed by people in B.C. and Quebec.

• Quebec and the Prairie residents are more likely than others to indicate uneasiness with Natives.

Nationally, differences by **age** and especially **gender** are fairly slight.

Feelings of Uneasiness Around Three Select Groups by Region, Age, and Gender

	Natives	EInds	Asians
BC	19%	7	5
Prairies	14	5	11
Ontario	11	5	5
Quebec	22	14	14
Atlantic	14	9	9
18-34	15	8	8
35-54	11	6	9
55+	21	11	8
Women	15	9	9
Men	16	7	8

THE LONGER LOOK

* In 1955, Gallup asked Canadians if they would approve or disapprove of having "a few families from Europe come to this neighbourhood to live." Of those offering a definite opinion, 56% said they would "approve."

* In 1995, I asked Canadians to respond to the statement, "I'd approve of having families from Asian countries come to live in my neighbourhood." This time, 85% said they would.

Interpersonal Relations

Canadians value good interpersonal life. Ideally, the Canada of the post-50s has been a place where social life has been improving, where ties with others for the most part are good and life can be lived without anxiety and fear.

Views of People

Some 8 in 10 of us say that most of the time people try to be both *"helpful and fair."* However, as noted earlier, we often think that other people don't share our values. In fact, about 80% of us say that the people we encounter, while often helpful and fair, still tend to be *"looking out for themselves."*

As a result, **we tend to be cautious.**

• Some 75% say *"one cannot be too careful in dealing with people,"* while an anxious 20% go so far as to say that *"a stranger who shows a person attention is probably up to something."*

• Among teenagers, the "stranger" figure is a whopping 40%.

PROJECT CANADA FAST-FACTS

The 1995 survey has found that substantial numbers of Canadians are convinced that, over the past five years, strangers have been changing.

	Decrease	Increase	No Change
Their friendliness	32%	10	58
Their helpfulness	31	9	60
Require caution	10	49	41

Fear

We are not just suspicious of each other; we're also frequently afraid of each other – but not much more than in the 70s.

Perhaps surprising to many, as prevalent as our concern about *crime and violence* may be today, that concern was even greater in 1975.

View as "Very Serious"		
	1975	1995
Crime	56%	46
Violence	50	35

Since the 1970s, there has been virtually no change in the proportion of Canadians who:

- express fear about walking alone at night,
- have been threatened with a gun or shot at,
- have had someone break into their homes, or
- have been forcibly robbed.

Fear and Victimization: 1975 Through 1995		1975	1980	1985	1990	1995
Is area within kilometre of home where afraid walk alone at night	Women	60%	60	60	52	63
	Men	21	19	21	20	21
Have been threatened with a gun or shot at in Canada	Women	2	3	6	5	5
	Men	7	7	7	10	6
In previous year, someone illegally entered apt or home	Women	7	11	7	9	7
	Men	9	8	9	7	5
In previous year, someone took something by using force	Women	2	2	4	3	3
	Men	2	2	5	3	3

This isn't to imply the levels are nott to be taken seriously. The good news is that the levels *haven't increased* in the past two decades. The bad news? They *haven't decreased*.

The fact that about 6 in 10 women – and 2 in 10 men – continue to express fear for their personal safety is sometimes grounded in personal experience.

For example, a total of 19% of Canadian women and 3% of men say that they have been sexually assaulted.

Such assaults are most readily acknowledged by almost equal proportions of women between the ages of 18 and 34 and 35 and 54, and most often by men who are 35 to 54.

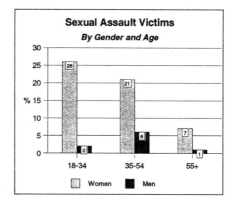

Sexual Assault Victims
By Gender and Age

In addition to reflecting what has actually been taking place, these differences also suggest both a growing inclination on the part of victims to disclose what has happened, as well as decreasing tolerance of such behaviour.

Fear and victimization tend to be greater in larger cities.

• However, for women, *fear* is high in virtually every size of community – especially those over 100,000, whereas for men, concern about personal safety tends to increase with city size.

• People who have been *sexually assaulted* are frequently residents of both larger and smaller cities; the survey, however, did not isolate where an assault took place. Some victims presumably have moved after such incidents, perhaps sometimes to larger cities, then again, sometimes to smaller areas.

• *Burglaries* in the last year are reported by people in all sizes of communities, with women particularly vulnerable in cities of 400,000 to 1 million; *robberies* are marginally higher in Toronto, Montreal, and Vancouver than elsewhere.

Fear and Victimization by Community Size

	FEAR		SEX ASSLT		BURGLAR		ROBBED	
	Women	Men	Women	Men	Women	Men	Women	Men
Over 1 million	73%	29	19	3	6	5	6	4
400,000-1 million	76	23	27	7	16	6	2	3
100,000-400,000	74	21	17	2	9	7	3	1
30,000-100,000	65	17	23	4	8	7	3	5
<30,000	49	15	17	3	5	4	1	2

TREND TRACKING

In the post-1950s we have been trying hard to improve social life in Canada. That should, ideally, translate into more freedom, more opportunity, more equality, more justice.

Attitudinally, our intergroup life has been improving fairly markedly during the last part of the century. While we still have a good distance to go, the vast majority of people are exhibiting increasing acceptance of cultural minorities and previously stigmatized categories. A fairly overt "bigoted core" of about 10% of the population still exists. Further, recent increases in negative attitudes toward some groups serve as a reminder that interpersonal attitudes and behaviour do not necessarily only change for the better, but rather can readily regress.

On a more general interpersonal level, we are often unsure of the values and intentions of others. Even though our trepidation about possible crime and violence seems greatly exaggerated, we proceed with extreme caution in relating to people generally and strangers specifically. We continue to experience a lot of interpersonal joy, but also a lot of interpersonal anxiety and fear.

THE PROJECT CANADA PANEL

	NO CHANGE	INCREASE	DECREASE	TOTALS
Approve Marriages				
Whites and Blacks				
Baby Boomers	83	11	6	100
Boomers' Parents	76	18	6	100
Crime Very Serious				
Baby Boomers	61	20	19	100
Boomers' Parents	61	17	22	100

6 - REEXAMINING SEXUALITY
What We Approve of With Whom

PROFOUND →

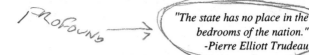

"The state has no place in the bedrooms of the nation."
-Pierre Elliott Trudeau

1965	Pope Paul VI reaffirms Catholic Church's opposition to birth control. The widely adopted "pill" had been introduced in 1960.
1970	Canadian Medical Association drops abortion from its code of ethics. Some 4,375 abortions performed in first year since crim code amended.
1975	Toronto passes regulations aimed at reducing number body rub parlours. Nat Parole Board refuses Morgentaler parole; serving 18-month sentence.
1980	United Church issues sexuality report; incl gays should be elig for ministry. Anglican General Synod refers issue of common-law marriages to Bishops.
1985	Govt-commissioned report says "the pill" might have serious side-effects. Bill passed making it illegal for prostitutes, customers to interact publicly.
1990	Court rules a homosexual couple not a family under fed workplace laws. Fed govt releases AIDS strategy; pledges $112 million over three years.
1995	Ontario judges clears Eli Langer's sexual art involving children. Ruling in Ontario clears way for same-sex couples to adopt children.

Since the 1950s, we have been conscious of the need to be more open about sexuality.

• We've been publicly discussing our values, behaviour, and responses on an array of topics – what's sexually appropriate, gay rights, sex education, and the legal availability of abortion.

• We also have attempted to come to grips with pornography, as well as how to deal with the ongoing reality of prostitution.

And of course, in the midst of all these heavy debates, the nation has continued to enjoy sex.

Sexual Behaviour

As of the mid-1990s, just over 1 in 2 Canadian adults say that they engage in sex at least once a week. Another 15% or so acknowledge that they have sex 2 to 3 times a month while 10% do so about once a month. The remaining one-quarter of the population are almost evenly divided between those who "hardly ever" engage in sex and those who say they never do.

Sexual Activity by Region
"About How Often Do You Engage in Sex?"

	Daily	Several Week	Once Week	2-3 Month	Once Month	Hardly Ever	Never	Totals
CANADA	**3%**	**25**	**25**	**14**	**9**	**13**	**11**	**100**
BC	5	25	26	15	4	13	12	100
Prairies	3	24	25	17	7	12	12	100
Ontario	5	19	26	14	9	17	10	100
Quebec	2	33	22	13	12	10	8	100
Atlantic	2	27	26	11	11	9	14	100

Regionally, people in Quebec appear to have sex more often than anyone (35% several times a week or more). They are followed in order by those living in B.C. and the Atlantic provinces (about 30%), and then by Prairie (27%) and Ontario residents (24%).

A PROJECT CANADA FAST-FACT
Since 1975, Canadians have consistently maintained that "birth control information should be available to teenagers who want it."
1975: 94%   1980: 95%   1985: 91%   1990: 95%   1995: 94%

Indicative of changing ideas about sex and marriage:

• Canadians who are *cohabiting* and unmarried, who tend to be somewhat younger, claim to be having sex more often than any category;

• 60% of married couples say they are having sex weekly or more;

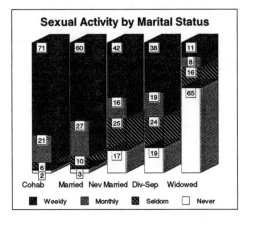

• 87% of single adults who have *never been married* acknowledge that they engage in sex , as do 81% of those people who are *divorced or separated;*

• around 35% of Canadians who are *widowed* and have not remarried are sexually involved on at least some occasions.

PROJECT CANADA FAST-FACTS

* As of 1995, 78% of Canadians indicate they approve of "an unmarried couple living together."
* The figure slips to 60% when it comes to their approving of "an unmarried couple having children."

As might be expected the most sexually active Canadians are men and women under the age of 40.

• From about 50 onward, men are more likely than women to say that they are having sex at least weekly. If those men and women are telling the truth, one is left with the obvious conclusion that many men over 50 are having sex with women under 50.

• Of interest, about 30% of people between the ages of 60 and 70, led by men, claim to be highly active.

• In fact, about 1 in 5 men and 1 in 15 women over the age of 70 say they're having sex weekly or more.

Such findings may shake up a stereotype or two about age and sex.

Sexual Activity by Gender and Age

		Weekly+	Never
18-29	Men	58%	4
	Women	66	5
30-39	Men	78	2
	Women	67	4
40-49	Men	60	3
	Women	58	7
50-59	Men	52	1
	Women	47	13
60-69	Men	30	5
	Women	25	41
70+	Men	22	25
	Women	7	58

There's also no little stereotyping when it comes to religion and sex. **Many think that religion inhibits sexual activity – even within marriage**. Some religious leaders respond that, in the context of good relationships, sex is to be fully embraced. Yet other leaders say it should be linked soley to procreation, with birth control possibilities fairly limited – a view that surely has some impact on incidence. So, what's really happening?

The 1995 survey shows that Catholics are reporting a higher level of sexual activity than Protestants and other faith groups.

• Canadians identifying with some of the conservative Protestant denominations – such as Baptists, Mennonites, and Pentecostals – are just as likely as Mainline Protestants to be having sex regularly.

• Slightly lower levels of sexual activity among some unmarried Mainline groups is due partly to the greater presence of older people.

𝔚𝔢𝔢𝔨𝔩𝔶 𝔖𝔢𝔵𝔲𝔞𝔩 𝔄𝔠𝔱𝔦𝔳𝔦𝔱𝔶
𝔅𝔶 𝔕𝔢𝔩𝔦𝔤𝔦𝔬𝔲𝔰 𝔊𝔯𝔬𝔲𝔭

	Married	All
ROMAN CATHOLIC	64%	56
PROTESTANT	54	46
Conservative	55	57
Mainline	53	45
Anglican	50	43
United Church	53	45
OTHER FAITHS	**	55
NONE	77	68

 Consistent with popular thinking, the highest level of sexual activity is claimed by people with *no religious affiliation*. The difference, however, has been overplayed.

• In part, it simply reflects the fact that "religious nones" are *slightly younger* than the affiliated and more frequently are not married.[1] A closer look at 18 to 34-year-olds who are married reveals little difference in the "amount" of sex being experienced by "nones" (78% weekly-plus) and those who identify with religious groups (72%).

Beyond identification, actual religious participation also is *not* associated with lower levels of sexual activity.

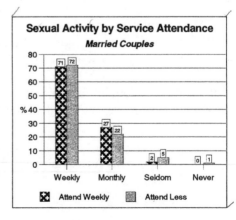

Sexual Activity by Service Attendance
Married Couples

Weekly: Attend Weekly 71, Attend Less 72
Monthly: Attend Weekly 27, Attend Less 22
Seldom: Attend Weekly 2, Attend Less 5
Never: Attend Weekly 0, Attend Less 1

■ Attend Weekly   ▨ Attend Less

Nonmarital Sex

The sexual revolution of the 60s has had a strong impact on attitudes and behaviour concerning sex outside of marriage.

• In 1975, just over 32% of Canadians tended to disapprove of premarital sex; since 1990, that figure has dropped to 20%.

• Today, almost 6 in 10 people say that premarital sex is "not wrong at all"; another 2 in 10 feel it's only "sometimes wrong."

Nonmarital Sexual Attitudes: 1975 Through 1995

	1975	1980	1985	1990	1995
Not wrong at all	39%	46	50	55	57
Sometimes wrong	29	28	27	25	23
Almost always wrong	13	10	8	7	7
Always wrong	19	16	15	13	13

The impact of "the revolution" can be seen in comparing age groups of the mid-70s with their counterparts today.

• In 1975, 90% of Canadians between the ages of 18 and 34 approved of premarital sex, in sharp contrast to 65% of people 35 to 54 and 42% of those 55-plus.

Approval of Premarital Sex by Age: 1975 and 1995

	1975	1995
NATIONALLY	68%	80
18-34	90	89
35-54	65	85
55 & over	42	62

• Today, the approval figure for 18 to 34-year-olds is about the same – 89%; but with aging, what was 65% in 1975 for 35 to 54-year-olds is now 85%; what was 42% for those 55 and over is now 62%.

These findings suggest that by about the year 2010, close to 85% of Canadians will approve of nonmarital sex, while a durable core of some 15% will continue to be opposed to such behaviour.

The sexual revolution has not just affected young adults. **Teenagers both approve of premarital sex and are putting their attitudes into action.**[2]

• Some 55% of 15 to 19-year-olds say they are sexually involved – a figure that has remained fairly steady since at least the early 80s.

• The "involved" include some 62% of males and 49% of females.

Teenagers today, however, appear to be better informed than their predecessors.

• Some 85% of young people 15 to 19 have taken sex education courses, compared to only 40% of Canadian adults.

• Close to 9 in 10 of these older teens say that they are fairly well informed about birth control, with three-quarters of those who are sexually involved claiming to be using some types of available devices.

The Longer Look

* In mid-1943, Gallup asked Canadians whether or not they approved of a course in sex education being given to students in high schools. Among those with an opinion, 84% said they approved.

* As of 1995, a slightly higher proportion, 89%, approve of sex education being offered in public schools.

While pollsters, academics, journalists and the rest of us continue to talk about "premarital sex," the fact of the matter is that many divorced and separated people are actually engaging in sex *between* marriages. **These days, sex outside of marriage typically is not just premarital but *intermarital*.**

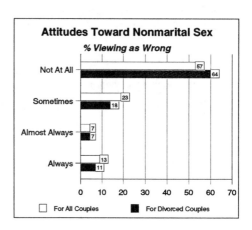

Attitudes Toward Nonmarital Sex

% Viewing as Wrong

	For All Couples	For Divorced Couples
Not At All	57	64
Sometimes	23	18
Almost Always	7	7
Always	13	11

We're even slightly more accepting of this kind of sex outside marriage, in all likelihood because it usually involves, not teens, but two consenting, sexually experienced adults.

AIDS

The survey findings suggest that the response of most singles to AIDS has been caution rather than abstinence.

• We've already seen that 87% of singles and 50% of older teenagers are engaging in sex.

• A full 40% of those same singles and 80% of teens see AIDS as a very serious problem, and large numbers say that it has led them and others to make changes in their sexual styles. Still, some 1 in 7 sexually involved single adults and 1 in 3

Perceived Changes in Sexual Habits Because of AIDS
Sexually Involved Singles

	Yes	Don't Know	No
Teens you know	33%	40	27
Adults you know	68	15	17
You yourself	84	--	16

teens admit that AIDS has **not** led them to alter their habits.

71

Homosexuality

Nationally, the level of acceptance of homosexuality has increased slowly but steadily since the 1970s.

• In 1975, 28% of Canadians said they regarded homosexual relations as either "not wrong at all" or "sometimes wrong."

• As of 1995, that figure has risen to 48%.

Attitudes Toward Homosexuality: 1975 Through 1995

	1975	1980	1985	1990	1995
Not wrong at all	14%	16	16	21	32
Sometimes wrong	14	14	13	13	16
Almost always wrong	10	8	9	7	7
Always wrong	62	62	62	59	45

The increase in the approval of homosexuality appears to reflect both a liberalization of attitudes among Boomers dating back to the 70s, and ongoing changes since then.

• In 1975, 18 to 34-year-olds held far more positive attitudes toward homosexuality than their parents and grandparents.

• They appear to have passed their views on to their children, while becoming somewhat more accepting of homosexuality themselves during the past 20 years; Boomers' Parents, on the other hand, collectively have changed little.

Approval of Homosexuality By Age: 1975 and 1995

	1975	1995
NATIONALLY	28%	48
18-34	42	59
35-54	25	54
55 & over	12	27

With the aging of our population, the approval level for homosexuality will pass 50% shortly after the turn of the century, and can be expected to reach about 60% in the forseeable future.

While half of the population does not approve of homosexuality, about three-quarters support the concept of extending civil and social rights to homosexuals.

• In 1980, some 70% said that "homosexuals are entitled to the same rights as other Canadians."

• That figure rose to 76% in 1985, reaching 80% in 1990.

How far people are willing to go in putting the idea of "same rights" into practice – such as providing same-sex benefits, extending adoption privileges, and so on – remains to be seen.

Significantly, between 1990 and 1995, during a time of considerable debate about same-sex rights, support for the idea of gays and lesbians receiving "the same rights as other Canadians" dropped from the 1990 high of 80% to 67%.

• It's clear that some lines are being drawn, not only with respect to spousal benefits, but also when it comes to access to some occupations.

• For example, as of 1995, a minority of 44% of Canadians agree that *"homosexuals should be eligible for ordination as ministers or priests."* The 1990 figure was 38%.

Homosexuals and Ordination *"Should Be Eligible"*	
NATIONALLY	**44%**
PROTESTANT	**39**
United Church	51
Anglican	46
Presbyterian	32
Lutheran	31
Baptist	28
ROMAN CATHOLIC	**34**
OTHER FAITHS	**53**
NONE	**84**

During the past two decades, there has a been a gradual increase in the inclination of Canadians to express feelings of being at ease in the presence of gays and lesbians. The "comfort levels" – as with their acceptance of homosexuality – have not matched their willingness to extend rights to homosexuals.

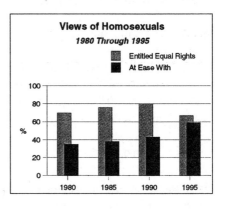

Ironically, just when Canadians are exhibiting both an increasing acceptance of homosexuality and greater social comfort with lesbians and gays, they now are also exhibiting *increasing discomfort* with the idea of extending them equal rights.

Extramarital Sex

In the 1960s and early 70s, the emphasis on sexual freedom was seen by some observers as transforming marriage.

• The traditional family, complete with exclusive partners, was being challenged by proponents of partner exchange ("swinging"), sexual freedom ("open marriage"), and even multiple marriage partners ("group marriage").

• Sociologists studying the family during that period genuinely didn't know how things would turn out by the end of the century.

Now we know. **The idea of having sex with someone other than one's marriage partner has failed to gain acceptance.**

• Reflecting the uncertain and flexible mood of the time, 22% of Canadian adults expressed the view in 1975 that sex *"with someone other than the marriage partner"* was either *"not wrong at all"* or only *"sometimes wrong."*

• Today that figure stands at 15%.

Attitudes Toward Extramarital Sex: 1975 Through 1995

	1975	1980	1985	1990	1995
Not wrong at all	5%	4	3	3	3
Sometimes wrong	17	17	16	13	12
Almost always wrong	28	26	26	22	25
Always wrong	50	53	55	62	60

The radical change anticipated by some never took place.

• Only 11% of current 18 to 35-year-olds hold such a view, down from 28% for that cohort in 1975.

• Among teens, the 1992 approval figure was 10%.

Approval of Extramarital Sex By Age: 1975 and 1995

	1975	1995
NATIONALLY	22%	15
18-34	28	11
35-54	23	21
55 & over	12	10

PROJECT CANADA FAST-FACTS

A controversial topic in the post-50s has been the distribution of pornographic materials.

	Adults Only	No Distribution	No Restrictions
1975	52%	34	14
1985	57	38	5
1995	56	39	5

Variations Across the Country

Since the 1970s, there have been significant increases in the approval of premarital sex and homosexuality in every region of the country.

• Quebeckers have the most liberal sexual attitudes in general, including their views of extramarital sex: as in 1995, 1 in 4 residents express approval.

• Quebec's approval level of homosexuality is matched by B.C.

• Prairie residents are less inclined than other Canadians to approve of premarital sex, and are joined by the Atlantic region in expressing the greatest disapproval of homosexuality.

Sexual Relations Approval by Region: 1975 and 1995

	Premarital 1975	Premarital 1995	Homosexual 1975	Homosexual 1995	Extramarital 1975	Extramarital 1995
NATIONALLY	**68%**	**80**	**28**	**48**	**21**	**15**
British Columbia	77	82	31	55	20	12
Prairies	57	71	24	37	15	14
Ontario	69	78	28	48	24	11
Quebec	72	88	32	55	26	24
Atlantic	57	80	17	39	12	9

PROJECT CANADA FAST-FACTS

Prostitution is not an issue Canadians have been seeing as particularly pressing.

* In 1985, just 20% rated prostitution as a "very serious" problem, in contrast to such issues as unemployment (78%), child abuse (51%), pollution (50%), crime (49%), drugs (47%), and sexual assault (43%).

* Before and since, respondents have been asked to cite issues they themselves regard as serious. In 1995, less than 1% mentioned prostitution.

Abortion

A widely held notion is that Canadians are split almost evenly into pro-life and pro-choice camps over the issue of the availability of legal abortion.

It's just not so. In fact, it's not clear that a majority of people have been members of either camp during the modern debate.

According to the 1995 survey:

• 95% of the populace agree that a pregnant woman should be able to have access to a legal abortion when her *health* is seriously endangered;

• some 9 in 10 favour the availability of a legal abortion when *rape* is involved, or when there is a strong chance of a serious *defect* in the baby.

These levels are virtually unchanged from 1975.

Areas of Convergence in Abortion Attitudes
1975 Through 1995

"Do you think it should be possible for a pregnant woman to obtain a LEGAL abortion if..."

	1975	1980	1985	1990	1995
Her own health is seriously endangered by the pregnancy	94%	95	92	95	95
There is a strong chance of serious defect in the baby	85	88	86	88	88
She became pregnant as a result of rape	86	86	86	90	89

Canadians who take a pro-life position to the point of being opposed to abortion of any kind make up a 10% minority in Canada. That's about the same figure as in the mid-1970s.

But the other 90% of Canadians are far from pro-choice. When the health of the mother or the unborn child is *not* involved, many Canadians have significant reservations.

• If, for example, an abortion is sought because of inadequate income, being single, or not wanting any more children, the support for a legal abortion drops to around 50% or less.

• Abortion for any reason – "on demand" – has the support of only 40% of Canadians.

Areas of Divergence in Abortion Attitudes
1975 Through 1995

"Do you think it should be possible for a pregnant woman to obtain a LEGAL abortion if..."

	1975	1980	1985	1990	1995
The family has a very low income and cannot afford more children	58%	55	52	55	54
She is not married and does not want to marry the man	49	51	48	48	48
She is married and does not want to have any more children	46	47	46	48	46
She wants it for any reason	**	**	37	38	39

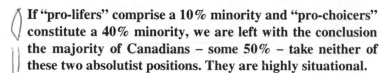

If "pro-lifers" comprise a 10% minority and "pro-choicers" constitute a 40% minority, we are left with the conclusion the majority of Canadians – some 50% – take neither of these two absolutist positions. They are highly situational.

78

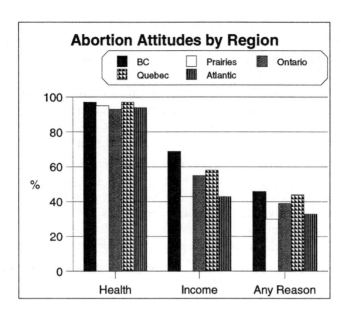

Abortion Attitudes by Region

Legend: BC, Quebec, Prairies, Atlantic, Ontario

And so it is that **regionally:**

• the vast majority of people right across the country have highly similar views about the availability of abortion when a mother's health is involved;

• however, people living in the Prairie and Atlantic regions are less likely than others to approve of the possibility of a legal abortion "on demand" or when the key issue is finances.

As we look to the immediate future, the prediction seems easy. **Abortion attitudes are not going to change very much.**

• There also are only small differences by *age* and *gender* and inconsistent patterns by *education* and *religious involvement.*

• As a result, aging, education, and secularization will not significantly alter the proportional sizes of the pro-life, pro-choice, and situational camps in at least the next few decades.

TREND TRACKING

The survey findings reveal that the sexual revolution has had a profound impact on Canada. What we have been witnessing is the transmission of the new sexual values from Baby Boomer revolutionists to their offspring. The protests of Boomers' Parents who were frequently troubled by the changes are increasingly a thing of the past.

While there has been a growing acceptance of homosexuality, little else has changed sexually since the 70s. "The Revolution" has long been over. Despite considerable debate, our views of sex outside of marriage, pornography, and abortion have remained remarkably steady, while we have reclaimed the views of parents and grandparents on extramarital sex. And, of course, like Canadians before us, we continue to enjoy sex.

As a society, we are not so much having to deal with what is "sexually new" as having to continue to find ways of accommodating our old sexual differences. We may well succeed in moving toward acceptance of our differences, developing something of a "moral mosaic." Then again, we may allow our sexual diversity to become another area of life that divides us.

THE PROJECT CANADA PANEL

	NO CHANGE	MORE POSITIVE	MORE NEGATIVE	TOTALS
Homosexuality				
Baby Boomers	53%	25	22	100
Boomers' Parents	69	14	17	100
Extramarital Sex				
Baby Boomers	52	14	34	100
Boomers' Parents	69	9	22	100

7 - REVITALIZING INDIVIDUALS
Our Primary Personal Concerns

1965	Unemployment under 6%. Daily male smokers about 52%, females 32%. Lone parent families 9.3% of all families. Contact lenses invented.
1970	Persons per nurse about 200, per physician over 700; per dentist over 3000. Programs and retail outlets stressing nutrition growing significantly.
1975	Federal health expenditures are 7.1% of gross domestic product. Families under poverty line 661,000. Average home resale $47,201.
1980	Supreme Court awards Rosa Becker half assets from common-law relship. Unemployment 7.5%. Fitness programs know burgeoning popularity.
1985	Fed govt addresses acid rain. Persons per nurse 130, per physician 487'; per dentist 1998. Leisure time 20% of day for emp men, 17% emp women.
1990	Daily male smokers 33%, females 29%. Packages to carry health warnings. Poverty families 769,000. Supreme Court upholds mandatory retirement.
1995	Unemployment 11%. Avg home sale about $150,000. Lone parents 13%. Court strikes down ban on TV liquor advertising. Health 10% of GDP.

Life's not exactly a breeze for anybody, even those who – on the surface – give us the impression that all is perfectly well.

• The experts tell us that people who are the happiest are those people who have realized that life is difficult.

• What makes these "happiest people" different is not that they don't have problems, but that they have learned how to respond to their problems.[1]

There's no utopia in sight. In the meantime, we all have to adjust. Some are responding better than others.

Our Foremost Concerns

On a personal level, there are three things that we say concern us the most: money, health, and time.

About half of us worry "a great deal" or "quite a bit" about the fact that we are not going to be able to have either the **financial** or **physical resources** to live life the way we would like.

And, even if we're lucky enough to have adequate dollars and still have our health, about half of us are troubled a fair amount by the fact that we don't have enough **time** to enjoy those valued resources.

Whatever happened to those relationships that supposedly are central to all that activity . . . Little wonder 1 in 3 of us say that we feel we **should be getting more out of life.**

Top 10 Personal Concerns

Concerned "A Great Deal" or "Quite a Bit"

1. Money	59%
2. Health	49
3. Time	48
4. Want more out of life	35
5. Children	35
6. Job	33
7. Lack of recognition	33
8. So much change	28
9. Loneliness	27
10. Sex life	27

Less Common

Marriage/relationship	26
Our looks	26
Getting older	21
Depression	19
Dying	16

• Just over 30% of people across the country, including 42% of those who are employed full-time, say that their **jobs** are a source of anxiety. For some, it's the work. For others, the prospect of *not* having stressful work is also stressful.

• Close to the same proportion of Canadians, representing 1 in 2 parents, say they worry about their **children**. Mothers and fathers worry about their children when they *are* children, and keep on worrying about them *long after* they are children. And parents with teenagers worry about their kids the most – but just barely.

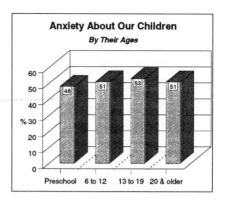

Anxiety About Our Children
By Their Ages

Age group	%
Preschool	48
6 to 12	51
13 to 19	53
20 & older	51

• Given how much we value relationships and being loved, it's not surprising that about 30% admit that, frankly, it would be nice to get more **recognition** for the things we do.

• Around 30% of us also acknowledge we are feeling a shade perplexed that "**so many things are changing.**" We might be doing a fairly good job of coping with change, but that isn't to say we wouldn't like a breather.

• Some 1 in 4 people across the country say that **loneliness** bothers them "a great deal" or "quite a bit"; they include 32% of people who are 55 and older, but also 28% of adults under the age of 35, and 32% of those who are 35 to 54.

• Another 1 in 4 Canadians worry about their **sex lives**, including about half of the people who also indicate that they are troubled about their **marriages or relationships**; people in the "troubled relationship category" number about 25%.

• **Further issues**, including *getting older, looks, depression, boredom, poor self-esteem,* and *dying,* are certainly important for some Canadians, but not most.

Our primary concerns have not changed much in recent years and, I suspect, in many years.

I often remind audiences of sociologist Gwynn Nettler's observation that people just about everywhere have two primary concerns: they want to stay alive and they want to live well.[2]

We're no different. That's why we keep saying that our foremost concerns pertain to the "staying alive" issue of health, and to the "living well" issues of money, time, recognition, and getting the most out of life.[3] In 1995, perhaps in part reflecting an aging population, living well has resulted in our expressing somewhat more concern about both health and our children.

Top Five Personal Concerns: 1980 Through 1995

1980	1985	1990	1995
Time	Money	Money	Money
Money	Time	Time	Health
More out life	Health	Recognition	Time
Recognition	More out life	More out life	More out life
Health	Recognition	Health	Children

Regionally, Quebeckers express more concern about just about everything than people elsewhere, whereas B.C. residents tend to express lower levels of concern particularly about money, health, and even time.

• While differences between **women and men** are minor, women tend to express more concern about lack of time.

• **Age-wise**, younger Canadians are more likely than others to express concern about *money, time*, and their *marriages and relationships*. Interestingly, when it comes to health and the inclination to be troubled that "so many things are changing," differences by age are fairly small.

Personal Concern Variations by Region, Gender, and Age
Concerned "A Great Deal" or "Quite a Bit"

	Money	Health	Time	Change	Marriage/ Relationships
NATIONALLY	**59%**	**48**	**49**	**28**	**29**
BC	46%	35	42	24	25
Prairies	52	43	41	27	24
Ontario	57	43	45	27	27
Quebec	74	67	64	31	35
Atlantic	58	55	38	36	30
Women	58	50	52	29	28
Men	60	49	45	27	30
18-34	71	50	55	26	33
35-54	59	44	51	28	29
55+	44	56	35	31	21

Some Further Reflections on Health, Time, and Marriage

Health

One of the obsessions of the post-1950s has been health and fitness. The 1990 national survey found that 91% of Canadians regarded "keeping fit" as "very" or "somewhat" important. As just seen, the 1995 survey has found that 1 in 2 people under the age of 35 say they are frequently concerned about their health.

More of us than ever before seem to be watching what we are eating and making efforts to be in good physical shape.

• Some 20% of Canadians claim that they are exercising every day, 70% every week; just 4% indicate they never exercise.

• A full 75% say they play sports, 50% at least once a month.

So what's it adding up to?

• In 1975, 79% of respondents described their health as either "excellent" or "good." The figure for 1995 is up slightly to 81%.

• There have been no noteworthy changes by *age* for men since the 70s. There has, however, been a slight tendency for *women 35 and older* to be *somewhat more positive* about their health than their cohort counterparts of two decades ago.

Self-Reported Health
Describe as "Excellent" or "Good"

	1975	1995
NATIONALLY	78%	82
Women	73	80
18-34	84	84
35-54	76	84
55+	58	63
Men	84	85
18-34	94	94
35-54	87	85
55+	66	68

Objectively, we may be healthier in the 90s than we were in the 70s. But subjectively, we are feeling pretty much the same.

This finding about "feeling healthy" is not insignificant. We know well that there's a strong relationship between what we think about our health and how we feel physically. And in the 70s, with far less emphasis on health and fitness, Canadians were thinking they were just as healthy as we think we are now.

A PROJECT CANADA FAST-FACT

The 1995 survey has found that 27% of Canadians took "a personal development course" during the past year. They include 34% of Boomers, 31% of Boomers' Kids, and 12% of Boomers' Parents.

The folk and medical wisdom is that "a good night's sleep" for most people is probably about 7 to 8 hours. In the light of living what we see as increasingly hectic lives, many of us might suspect we're contributing to a decline in the national average.

• Maybe. But the 1995 survey has found that almost 50% of Canadians say they sleep *at least 8 hours* a night, including 10% for whom 9 hours-plus is the norm.

• Another 30% get about *7 hours'* sleep on average.

• Just 20% of us tend to get *less than 7 hours'* sleep.

• Some 60% of **men** say they sleep less than 8 hours a night, compared to 50% of **women**.

• As for **age**, Boomers (between the ages of 35 and 54) are the least likely of any age group to be getting at least 8 hours of sleep a night.

Boomer men seem to be particularly hard pressed for sleep, with only 23% averaging 8 hours or more, considerably below the national average of 43%.

How Many Hours of Sleep We Are Getting

	<7	7	8	9+
ALL	24%	33	34	9
Women	25	26	40	9
18-34	23	25	41	11
35-54	27	32	35	6
55+	26	18	44	12
Men	23	40	29	8
18-34	22	37	32	9
35-54	26	51	20	3
55+	21	30	37	12

The Longer Look

* **We seem to be going to bed a bit later.**

In 1945, Gallup found that 31% of Canadians were in bed by 10 p.m., 71% by 11, and 94% by midnight; as of 1995, only 24% of us had "hit the sack" by 10, 67% by 11, and 92% by 12.

* **We also seem to be going to doctors a bit more often.**

In 1995, 81% of us said we'd been to a physician in the past year, while 68% had seen a dentist; in 1950, Gallup found that 64% of Canadians had been to a physician and 52% to a dentist in the previous 12 months.

Time

Although undoubtedly many Canadians have always felt that they didn't have enough time, those sentiments have increased greatly in recent years.

• The contributions of technology have accelerated expectations about quality and have decimated time-lines.

• Fax machines and E-mail, laptops and software, portable printers and cellular phones have taken away our hiding places and our excuses for not producing immediate turnarounds.

Asked about trends over the past five years:

• 7 in 10 women and men say that *"the general pace of life"* has been increasing, as have the *demands on their time*;

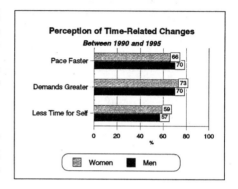

• close to the same number report having less time for themselves; and

• 6 in 10 say there's been a decrease in *the time they have to do the things they want.*

Those levels, incidentally, are slightly below those of 1990, despite our perception that, time-wise, things are worse.

PROJECT CANADA FAST-FACTS

In 1995, 76% of Canadians said they had taken a vacation in the last year. By income bracket, they included approximately:
* 90% of people with family incomes of $60,000 or more;
* 80% with incomes between $40,000 and $59,000;
* 70% of people with incomes between $20,000 and $39,000; and
* 50% of people with family incomes under $20,000.

• In the mid-90s, 60% of us are saying we "almost never" have extra time on our hands that we "don't know what to do with." At best, 40% think such a situation exists "now and then," versus "quite often."

Women 35 and over are more likely than their male counterparts to say they don't have extra time, especially if they are employed full-time.

Almost Never Have Extra Time		
	Women	**Men**
NATIONALLY		
1995	63%	59
1990	67	66
18-34	49	58
35-54	75	62
55+	65	58
Employed full-time	70	62
Not emp full-time	58	55

Marriage

We've already seen that close to 90 to 95% of Canadians who are married indicate that they are reasonably happy with their marriages. The down side is that, at any point in time, perhaps about 1 in 10 are not very happy.

• In fact, more than 1 in 4 people who are married admit that they are concerned about their marriages, not necessarily always, but still "a great deal" (14%) or "quite a bit" (15%). Some of these won't stay together.

• Significantly, whereas just 4% of Canadians who are 55 and over say their parents were divorced or separated when they were 16, that figure has jumped to 18% for people under 35.

Yet, of considerable importance, most people don't give up on marriage. One in 5 might divorce. But most remarry.

Currently, about 10% of Canadians who are married have been married at least twice. Incidentally, some 23% of those people who are cohabiting have been married; the vast majority – some 75% – have never officially "tied the knot."

How do the lives of remarried Canadians compare with those people who are experiencing first-time marriages? An examination of a number of items from the 1995 survey provide us with some general findings on happiness and children.

First-time Marriages and Remarriages Correlates								
	Happy Marriage		Worry Marriage		Enjoy Children		Worry Children	
Mod	High	Mod	High	Mod	High	Mod	High	Mod
First-time	48%	47	12	13	76	19	22	26
Remarriages	41	54	8	17	77	14	27	27

• There are only small differences in the inclination to report marital happiness or marital strain. While some marriages in both categories won't last, at any given point in time the "happiness snapshots" are very similar.

• There are only slight differences between the remarried and first-time married when it comes both to enjoyment of children as well as the tendency to worry about them.

The Longer Look						
Ideal number of children according to Project Can95 and Gallup in 1945.						
	One	Two	Three	Four	Five-Plus	Totals
1995	2%	53	29	12	4	100
1945	<1	17	23	31	29	100

TREND TRACKING

In the post-1950s, our society has been engaged in a vigorous effort both to recognize personal concerns and respond to them. These have been years when considerable emphasis has been given to addressing economic issues, finding ways of saving time, and focusing as never before on health and fitness. More and more advocacy groups have been drawing attention to problems, and growing numbers of specialists have been appearing to deal with them.

The net result is that we think we are doing pretty well emotionally and relationally. In that regard, we are essentially on a par with the self-images of previous Canadian generations. Since the early 80s, however, growing numbers of people have been more troubled than our parents and grandparents about what is happening to them financially.

We consequently have become increasingly critical of our society and our leaders, which brings us to our next chapter.

THE PROJECT CANADA PANEL

	SAME	BETTER	WORSE	TOTALS
Financial Trends				
Baby Boomers	32%	4	64	100
Boomers' Parents	37	12	51	100
Health				
Baby Boomers	50	9	41	100
Boomers' Parents	53	8	39	100

8 - READDRESSING ISSUES
Our Primary Social Concerns

"We have to concentrate all our efforts
on the economy, to create jobs."
-Jean Chrétien, victory speech, 1993

1965	Population hits 20 million, almost double 1941. Autopact signed with U.S. PM Pearson criticizes American role in Vietnam. Draft-dodgers appearing.
1970	FLQ kidnaps Cross, murders Laporte; Trudeau invokes War Measures Act. Status of Women report tabled. Olsen arrested for multiple murders in B.C.
1975	Federal government imposes wage and price controls for three-year period. Three New York-bound jets from Europe hijacked. Petro-Can created.
1980	Quebec votes "no" in referendum. Bank of Canada rate hits record 17.36%. National Energy Program created, Alberta outraged. Iran-Iraq war begins.
1985	Bank of Canada rate hits seven-year low of 9%. South Africa sanctioned. Police seeking leads in murders of eight infants at Toronto hospital.
1990	Meech fails. Standoff at Oka. Soviet bloc breaks up. Germany reunited. Iraq invades Kuwait. Citizens' Forum established. GST becomes law.
1995	Largest retailer Dylex to close 200 stores, lay off 2,400. Unemp 9-10%. V-E anniversary; Hiroshima remembered. Quebec referendum revisited.

Our pursuit of the good life isn't carried out in isolation. What's been taking place in our broader Canadian social environment clearly has a critical impact on our ability to live life the way we want. We haven't liked everything that's been happening.

In the post-1950s, we've been extremely conscious of social problems that need to be addressed. In reality, the issues are so numerous that they literally "compete" for attention and resources. As one observer once put it, "The number of serious social problems we will have at any one time will be limited by the size of the front page of the newspaper." Today, we could just as readily say "the length of the news telecast."

With the explosion of television channels, an unprecedented number of social issues have been receiving attention in the last part of this century. The greater presence of women in the media has also influenced what issues are given what play.

In the end, media exposure and personal experience result in our having strong feelings about which issues deserve priority.

The three issues that concern Canadians the most all have to do with money: the national debt, unemployment, and the economy. It is also clear where most lay the blame: **government incompetence.**

• Right behind these "living well" issues are four "staying alive" concerns: **crime, delinquency** (defined in Canada, of course, by *the Young Offenders Act*), **child abuse**, and **AIDS**.

Top 10 Social Concerns View as "Very Serious"	
1 The national debt	72%
2. Unemployment	55
3. The economy	54
4. Crime	46
5. Govt incompetence	45
6. Child abuse	43
7. AIDS	41
8. Juvenile delinquency	39
9. Family breakdown	36
10. Violence	35

• Two other key issues are **family breakdown** and **violence**.

A number of issues that receive considerable publicity and official attention are not viewed as severe problems by as many as 1 in 5 people.

As of the summer of 1995, **lack of unity is viewed by only 24% of Canadians as a "very serious" problem.**

Some Other Social Concerns View as "Very Serious"	
Racial discrimination	14%
Inequality of women	16
French-English relations	17
Sexual harassment	17
Native-White relations	18

♀ PROJECT CANADA FAST-FACTS

* Since the mid-1970s, there's been a shift in attitudes toward women.

"AGREE"	1975	1995
Women who do the same work as men should not necessarily receive the same pay.	9%	5
Married women should not be employed if their husbands are capable of supporting them.	34	10
Women should take care of running their homes and leave running the country up to the men.	22	10
Women have sufficient power in the nation's affairs.	47	63

* Re: an age-old stereotype: in 1945, Gallup found that 45% of Canadians thought women were worse drivers than men; today that figure is 10%.

Since the 1970s, the key issues that have preoccupied average Canadians have been the economy, unemployment, and crime.

Top Five Social Concerns: 1975 Through 1995

1975	1980	1985	1990	1995
Economy	Economy	Unemp	Economy	National debt
Crime	Crime	Economy	Environment	Unemp
Violence	Unemp	Child abuse	Govt income	Economy
Unemp	Violence	Pollution	GST	Crime
Drugs	Drugs	Crime	Child abuse	Govt income

Beyond asking respondents how seriously they regard a wide variety of issues, since 1985 I've also asked them what they consider to be the country's no. 1 problem. The top two winners by a landslide in both 1985 and 1995 were *the economy* and *unemployment*. In 1990, they had to share top billing with *government incompetence* and *lack of leadership*.

There are some important differences by region and community size.

• **Regionally,** *unemployment* is a particular concern in Quebec and the Atlantic provinces, but differences are not very great when it comes to both *crime* and *youth offences*. Prairie and Atlantic residents are somewhat less troubled than others about *the environment*, as well as *the need for gun controls*. **Concern about unity is highest, not in Quebec, but in Ontario**.

• As for **community size**, concern about crime and youth offences is somewhat lower in Vancouver, Toronto and Montreal collectively than in other communities – perhaps, in part, because such activity is regarded as fairly "normal." However, people in those three cities lead the nation in calling for gun controls. Variations by community size and issues such as unemployment, the environment, and unity are slight.

Select Concerns by Region and Community Size
View as "Very Serious"

	Unemp	Crime	Day	Envmt	Unity	Gun Controls
NATIONALLY	**55%**	**46**	**39**	**33**	**25**	**30**
BC	38	51	39	34	23	22
Prairies	44	49	44	27	23	14
Ontario	54	41	40	37	30	34
Quebec	67	49	36	29	22	42
Atlantic	68	48	39	40	22	19
1 Million +	51	38	31	36	22	40
400,000-1M	58	47	35	36	26	25
100,000-400T	58	43	40	38	28	27
30,000-100,000	58	50	49	36	23	37
Less 30,000	54	50	42	29	27	24

Canadians also differ somewhat in their concern about certain social issues, depending on their gender and age.

• More *women* than men express concern about almost every issue, especially those with an explicit personal focus – unemployment, for example, versus unity.

• *Age* differences are minor with respect to most issues; Canadians who are 55 and over are slightly more concerned than others about crime and unity.

Select Concerns by Gender and Age
View as "Very Serious"

	Unemp	Crime	Day	Envmt	Unity	Gun Controls
NATIONALLY	55%	46	39	33	25	30
Women	64	51	48	39	25	38
Men	46	41	31	28	25	23
18-34	52	42	43	35	25	32
35-54	58	42	36	35	21	28
55+	56	56	40	29	32	31

Some Reflections on Employment, Youth, and Unity

Employment

The ability to have a comfortable life obviously requires that people have paid **work. The necessity of work means that the inability to find a paid job often represents a major crisis.**

Since at least the end of the Second World War, jobs and careers have been vigorously pursued not only by men but increasingly by women.

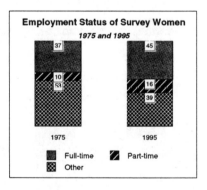

Employment Status of Survey Women
1975 and 1995

37 45

10 16
53 39

1975   1995

■ Full-time   ▨ Part-time
▩ Other

Combined with a big jump in divorce rates and changing family structures, **the movement of women into the paid work force has meant that tough economic times have had particularly pronounced personal and social consequences.** Women, men, children, and society have all been affected.

The uncertainty of the economy in recent years, along with other factors including increasing global competition, free trade, and mind-boggling and occupation-altering technological advances, have combined to make jobs unstable and careers short.

What the 1995 survey shows is that while large numbers of people who are employed are enjoying their jobs, they also are frequently experiencing considerable strain. Such anxiety is equally characteristic of both women and men who are employed full-time.

• About 1 in 6 Canadians currently employed full-time say that they switched jobs in the last year alone.

• While some 74% of full-timers say they *enjoy* their jobs, no less than 42% say that having and keeping them results in their worrying a "great deal" or "quite a bit" about them.

Experiences and Attitudes of Canadians Employed Full-time

	Switched Last Year	Enjoy Job	Concern About
CANADA	17%	74	42
Women	14	77	45
Men	18	71	40

As we have already seen, **women employed full-time are more likely than other women or men to say they are short on time.** One obvious reason is that they still are having to work "double days" – putting in time at work, and then coming home and doing much of the work on the domestic front as well.

After initially monitoring attitudes toward women *being in* the paid work force, **I've been focusing some attention in recent years on what happens when women *come home* from that work force**. My expectation has been that male companions increasingly are sharing the workload when both are employed.

In a very large number of cases, it still isn't happening.
Respondents have been asked about the division of labour
between themselves and their partners with respect to "things
like cooking, cleaning, and laundry." Where both have been
employed full-time:

• in 1990, 50% said that "she" either does all of it or most of it;
46% indicated the work is shared; just 4% said "he" does all or
most of it.

• as of 1995, 44% say that "she" is still doing all or most, 53%
claim the work is shared, and in 3% of the cases, that "he" is
carrying most of the load.

That's not a lot of change, but it may be a preview of more
significant developments.

In situations where both
partners are employed
full-time and are under
the age of 40, 62% say
the housework is being
shared; where the two
people are 40 or older,
the figure is just 45%.
Still, more than 1 in 3
women who work for
pay are carrying an ex-
cessive workload.

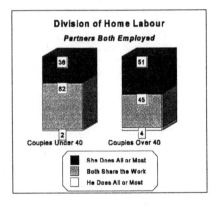

Division of Home Labour
Partners Both Employed

36
62
2
Couples Under 40

51
45
4
Couples Over 40

■ She Does All or Most
▨ Both Share the Work
□ He Does All or Most

PROJECT CANADA FAST–FACTS

In situations where both partners are employed full-time and at least one
preschool child is present, 36% of women do all or most of the housework. Where no preschoolers are present, the figure is 46%.

Youth

There currently is considerable concern about young people. Some 4 in 10 Canadians see *"juvenile delinquency"* – a term intended to embrace a wide range of youth offences – as a "very serious problem."

There are *additional signs* we are troubled about young people.

• Some 31% believe violence at schools has become a severe problem.

• The view of 74% that *"values have been changing for the worse"* often seems to be held with young people in mind.

Close to 1 in 10 people say they would feel uneasy around a person, if the only thing they knew about them was that they were a teenager.

Not high,you say? If you are a teenager, that translates into 1 in 10 people who may act awkward around you in a mall, on the bus, on a sidewalk, in a store. It's slightly higher than the proportion who say they initially feel uneasy around Jews.

As we have seen, concern about young people varies little across the country.

• About 40% of the residents in every region view the issue as "very serious." Concern is slightly higher in smaller cities.

• While concern is greater among women than men, it is shared almost evenly by people of all ages.

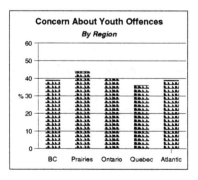

As concerned as Canadians are about young people these days, it's important not to lose perspective. **Concern about young people seems to characterize every generation, who anxiously envision that "the latest crop" will turn out worse than the last one.**

Today's level of concern about youth is almost identical to what it has been since at least 1975. The only time concern dropped noticeably in the past two decades was around 1990, when our attention was focused on other alleged crises, such as Meech Lake.

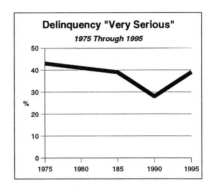

The Longer Look

* In the spring of 1955, the Gallup organization indicated that it had put an item to Canadians that read, "There's been a lot of discussion recently about our teenagers getting out of hand." People were asked for their opinions as to why teens were "acting up." That teen cohort, of course, was comprised of the older brothers and sisters of today's Baby Boomers.

* In 1965, Gallup found it pertinent to revisit the same issue. The teenage cohort that was the focus at that point? Baby Boomers.

As I've been emphasizing, the fact an issue has been a concern in the past in no way minimizes its significance in our day. But it does guard against both hyperbole and hysteria. It also means we might be able to learn from what has been tried before.

The obvious question that arises out of all this concern about young people is how to respond.

• Clearly, large numbers of Canadians think the onus lies on the home. Parents, say 86%, should be *far stricter* with their children, with sentiments highly pervasive across the country.

• About 60% feel that it would wise to get young people under the age of 16 right off the streets at night, unless they are out with their parents.

Curfew sentiments are held by only about 50% of Quebeckers and are most popular in smaller communities and among older and younger adults.

Concern About Youth Across the Country	SCHOOL VIOLENCE	PARENTS NOT STRICT	WANT CURFEW
Canada	**31%**	**86**	**62**
BC	26	87	65
Prairies	31	88	63
Ontario	32	87	67
Quebec	34	82	49
Atlantic	29	90	72
Million +	32	85	58
400T-1M	30	87	47
10T-400T	33	82	59
30T-99T	28	88	64
Less 30T	33	88	69
Women	38	84	65
Men	24	88	59
18-34	31	87	62
35-54	28	83	57
55+	35	90	71

The Longer Look

* As part of that 1955 release on young people, Gallup reported, "The average man and woman puts the blame for teenagers acting up on the home, and parental discipline." The polling firm found that 81% of Canadians felt "discipline in most homes is not strict enough."

* In 1965, 81% said the same thing about how parents were handling teenage Baby Boomers.

The behavioural problems that characterize some young people today may, in part, be tied to how they have been raised. For what it's worth, the discipline experiences of Boomers' Children have been quite different from their Boomer Parents, and, in turn, their grandparents.

Here a comparison with earlier Gallup work is particularly helpful. In their spring 1955 survey dealing with youth, Gallup asked adults to look back to when they themselves were teenagers and indicate *"what kinds of punishment seemed to work best on children your age who refused to behave."*

• About 30% cited "whipping," 20% the taking away of privileges, 15% being kept at home, and just under 10% being "given a good talking to." Other factors made up some 25%.

I put the same question to Canadians in 1995, modifying the wording slightly to read, *"What kind of response seemed to work best on people your age who misbehaved?"*

• Some 30% cited the taking away of privileges, 40% being "given a good talking to," and 10% being grounded. Just 10% indicated "physical discipline"; 10% mentioned other factors (other, 8%).[4]

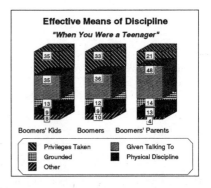

Effective Means of Discipline
"When You Were a Teenager"

Boomers' Kids — Boomers — Boomers' Parents

Privileges Taken · Grounded · Other · Given Talking To · Physical Discipline

---

THE LONGER LOOK

Incidentally, Gallup found in the 1955 poll that 81% of Canadians favoured *a curfew* for young people 16 and under.

There's little doubt that younger adults claim that parents are "doing more talking" and being far less physical in disciplining their children. Whether such a change is a key source of more youth and adult crime – over against our collective failure to instill positive interpersonal values, for example – is not clear.

What *is* clear, however, is that Canadians are extremely dissatisfied with *the Young Offenders Act*. The Act was passed in 1984 and responds to behaviour among young people between the ages of 12 and 17 which, if engaged in by adults, would be considered criminal. Additional kinds of behaviour, such as truancy and incorrigibility, are also addressed in the Act.

No less than 95% of Canadians maintain that *"the Young Offenders Act needs to be toughened."* **There are few topics and issues in the country that can begin to match such national unanimity.**

Unity

Canadian unity is a strange issue, in that it receives enormous political and media play yet fails to be viewed by a majority in Quebec or anywhere else as constituting a primary social problem.

As just noted, as of mid-1995, only 25% of the nation view *"the lack of Canadian unity"* as a "very serious" problem, compared, for example, to 72% who hold such a view of the national debt.

• In 1990, at the height of the Meech Lake debate and media declarations that the country was in crisis, just 37% of Canadians felt the lack of unity represented a "very serious" problem, compared to 57% for the economy. Further, only 26% gave the same severity rating to "the need for constitutional agreement."

• In 1980, on the heels of the 1976 election of the Parti Québécois and an imminent Quebec separation referendum, just 32% of Canadians expressed the sentiment that unity represented a "very serious" national issue; by 1985, the figure had dipped to 19%.

Concern about *French-English relations* more specifically has also fluctuated since the 60s, peaking around 1980 and 1990 with constitutional matters. But concern has not topped 40% for either Quebec residents or people in the rest of Canada.

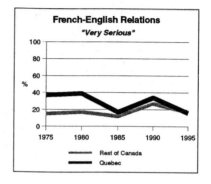

Indicative of the potential for conflict, Quebeckers and other Canadians continue to disagree about the respective amounts of *power* they have in the nation's affairs.

• Residents of Quebec have been feeling they don't have enough power, that others have too much.

• People elsewhere continue to sense that they have about the right amount of power, and that it's Quebeckers who have too much.

Perception of Power 1975, 1985, 1995				
	FRENCH CANADIANS		ENGLISH CANADIANS	
	Too Much	Too Little	Too Much	Too Little
QUEBEC				
1995	5 %	65	30	25
1985	4	59	35	16
1975	5	70	62	7
REST OF CANADA				
1995	57	9	7	32
1985	35	9	9	17
1975	43	10	9	22

Rather than views of power converging over time, as hoped for by the Liberals of the 60s, they have become more divergent in every **region**.

Increases in the perception of excessive French-Canadian power are most pronounced in both B.C. and Ontario.

Views of French Canadian Power

		Too Much	Too Little	About Right
BC	1995	60%	6	34
	1975	44	9	47
Prairies	1990	63	6	31
	1975	59	7	34
Ontario	1995	55	11	34
	1975	36	10	54
Atlantic	1995	48	13	39
	1975	40	12	48

As for "the big unity question" – Quebec's future – thoughts are varied.

• Approximately 80% of Canadians in the *rest of the country* feel Quebec will stay in the country.

• In *Quebec*, most Anglophones think the province will stay, but Francophones – by a slight margin – think the province will leave; the sovereignty-association possibility is third.

What Quebec Will Do
"Do you think that Quebec will..."

	STAY	SOV ASSOC	LEAVE
REST	81%	7	12
BC	80	8	12
Prairies	74	11	15
Ontario	86	4	10
Atlantic	80	7	13
QUEBEC	41	19	40
Francophone	35	21	44
Anglophone	87	4	9

PROJECT CANADA FAST-FACTS

French Canadians will gain world influence by the year 2000.

1975 - 31%; 1980 - 33%;

1985 - 29%; 1990 - 33%   1995 - 23%

TREND TRACKING

As with personal issues, social concerns are seldom new since they are related to what we all want most out of life. We've seen from the outset that we are explicit about valuing happiness and freedom, relationships and a comfortable life above everything else.

And so it is that the social problems we continue to define as being the most urgent are those that represent barriers to the resources and social and physical environments we want. Accordingly, unemployment and crime have always been among our central concerns. These core issues are readily supplemented by additional matters – some that affect us directly, some that affect others and call for our response.

In addressing social issues, we find ourselves having to depend on a wide variety of people in a wide variety of spheres. The survey findings indicate that, as of the mid-90s, we're feeling more than a little upset with more than a few of the people we are counting on. That's the topic we want to turn to next.

THE PROJECT CANADA PANEL

Seriousness of:	NO CHANGE	NOW HIGHER	NOW LOWER	TOTALS
Unemployment				
Baby Boomers	47%	38	15	100
Boomers' Parents	46	43	11	100
Crime				
Baby Boomers	52	23	25	100
Boomers' Parents	55	19	26	100

9 - REASSESSING LEADERSHIP
How We View Our Institutions and Leaders

"People wielding great power must be
held responsible for how they wield it."
-Keith Spicer

1965	Liberals form minority govt under Pearson; Trudeau elected to Commons. Large growth in universities & enrollments. Churchill dies. Marcos elected.
1970	Bill dealing with young offenders introduced. "Dief" celebrates 30 years. Trudeau establishes diplomatic relations with China. Cable TV arriving.
1975	Barbara Frum, 36, receives Press Club award for outstanding journalism.. Broadbent, 39, elected NDP head. TV cameras allowed in the Commons.
1980	Trudeau's Liberals oust Clark govt. Jeanne Sauvé first female Speaker. Quebec liberals defeat Levesque and P.Q. Medical extra-billing an issue.
1985	Marshall McLuhan dies. Premiers Levesque, Lougheed, Davis step down. Gorbachev becomes Soviet leader; meets with former PM Trudeau.
1990	Dollar steady after Meech failure. Bertha Wilson retires. Bouchard quits. Mount Cashel probe ends. Mulroney stacks senate. Mandela freed.
1995	Courts, police scrutinized in Bernardo &Simpson trials. Pro sports strike. Educ reforms widespread. Media mergers. Airborne Regiment disbanded.

In the decades since the 60s, we've been taking a new look at the major institutions that have an impact on our lives. These have been decades of accelerated individualism, accompanied by a growing awareness that we have limited resources on the one hand and a growing number of choices on the other.

Consequently we have become more demanding of institutions such as government, education, business, health, media, religion, and leisure. We don't hold them in awe; we have come to expect performance and accountability.

INSTITUTIONAL authority

In the mid-90s, we are showing an inclination to have decreasing confidence in leadership in just about every sphere of life.

• In only one area do more than 50% of Canadians indicate they have *"a great deal"* or *"quite a bit"* of confidence in leadership – **policing**. Yet even here there has been a slight drop since 1985.

• Since the 1980s, the levels of confidence in other areas of life have tended either to decrease or to plateau at about 40%.

Confidence in Leadership Have "A Great Deal" or "Quite a Bit"			
	1985	1990	1995
The Police	75%	70	68
Schools	49	55	44
Radio	**	52	40
Financial institutions	**	42	40
Major business	**	42	38
Newspapers	40	43	38
Religious groups	51	36	36
The court system	49	43	35
Your local government	**	28	33
Television	44	56	30
The federal government	30	13	25
Your provincial govt	31	30	22
The movie industry	**	**	20
Labour unions	21	26	19

In 1979, Gallup found confidence levels for schools to be 54%, major corporations 34%, religious groups 60%, and labour unions 25%.

-15% (+12) 50% 5%

DECREASING CONFIDENCE IN AUTHORITY/INSTITUTIONS

• The biggest confidence losers have been **television** and **radio**, along with the **court system** and **schools**.

• The confidence drop in the **federal government** and **religious organizations** appears to have bottomed out in 1990. In fact, federal and **local governments** have actually experienced modest gains in confidence in the past five years.

• Confidence levels for leaders associated with **newspapers**, **major business**, **financial institutions**, and **labour unions** have remained fairly steady.

Such specific findings are consistent with the population's general assessment of leadership in Canadian life. No less than 7 in 10 Canadians say that lack of leadership is a "very serious" (34%) or "fairly serious" (36%) national problem, similar to what it was five years ago, and just slightly below what it was five years ago when the federal government's popularity was at an all-time low.

The federal government's jump in confidence in reality represents an increase from extremely low – 13% in 1990 – to a moderately low 25% today.

• In 1990, only 19% of the Project Canada respondents agreed with the statement, "Mulroney is doing a pretty good job as Prime Minister."

• In sharp contrast, the 1995 survey has found that 65% of Canadians are willing to assign the "pretty good job" designation to Jean Chrétien.

Yet, the overall confidence level in federal government leaders as a whole remains fairly low. Based on the patterns of the past ten years, it can be expected at best to stay considerably below 40%, and at worst to head back down to below 20%.

The Longer Look

* Despite growing disillusionment with educational leaders, 74% of Canadians have indicated in the 1995 survey that, "Overall, public school teachers are very competent."

* In 1950, Gallup found that 80% of the population felt "public school teachers are as capable as they should be."

There are some important variations by both region and age in the confidence respondents have in leadership.

• **Regionally,** *Quebec* residents express higher levels of confidence in leadership in all areas, except for the provincial government. *Prairie* respondents are "higher" on their provincial governments than people elsewhere. *B.C.* residents tend to exhibit the least amount of confidence in leaders generally.

• **Age-wise,** *younger adults* are somewhat more critical of business and government, but less critical of the media.

• The overall disenchantment with leaders is so pervasive that there are virtually no significant differences in confidence in leadership by both **gender** and **education**.

Confidence in Leadership by Region and Age
Have "A Great Deal" or "Quite a Bit"

	BUSINESS	SCHOOLS	PAPERS	PROV	MOVIES
NATIONALLY	**38%**	**44**	**39**	**22**	**23**
BC	31	35	29	14	9
Prairies	36	48	30	37	10
Ontario	33	37	34	17	16
Quebec	49	54	53	23	39
Atlantic	37	50	42	24	17
18-34	34	40	47	18	27
35-54	37	46	33	23	16
55+	43	46	33	25	14
Female	35	43	34	21	21
Male	40	45	42	23	19
A degree or more	37	44	39	19	20
Post-secondary	38	41	38	21	23
High school or less	38	47	37	26	18

As Canada has moved into the so-called Information Age during the second half of this century, power relations have been changing. **Not everyone is happy with the emerging amounts of power that certain institutions and groups of people have been attaining.**

• There has been a sense on the part of 70-80% that *rich people* and *corporations* have far too much power in national life – but the perception has been declining.

• A steady 65-75% have been feeling the same about *politicians* and 60% about the *media.*

Those With "Too Much Power" *1975 Through 1995*					
	1975	80	85	90	1995
The rich	80%	82	74	77	74
Corporations	83	84	73	72	69
Politicians	**	70	65	76	63
The Media	**	54	52	58	59
Labour unions	74	79	66	54	59
Americans	72	61	52	58	54
Lawyers	**	49	**	**	50
Interest groups	**	**	**	27	45
Religious gps	**	20	20	28	27
Professors	**	14	**	**	10
Avg Canadians	**	**	**	<1	<1

• Around 60% also have seen *labour unions* and *Americans* as having excessive power in Canada, but the numbers in both cases have declined since the early 80s.

• *Lawyers* and *interest groups* also are viewed by about 1 in 2 Canadians as having too much power, with the jump significant in just the last five years for interest groups.

• *Religious leaders* are seen by about 3 in 10 people as having excessive power in national life, *academics* by only 1 in 10.

Of interest and significance, **less than 1% feel the infamous "average Canadian" has too much power in national affairs.** About 80% think that average people have "too little."

The Longer Look

*In 1950, Gallup found that 72% of Canadians felt the RCMP had about "the right amount" of power, 23% that it had "too little."

*As of 1995, 59% of our Project Canada respondents think that "the Mounties" have appropriate power, while 31% think they should have more. Only 10% feel they have "too much" power, versus 5% in 1950.

Some Further Reflections on the Justice System, Politicians, and the Media

The Justice System

Despite the fact the police have come under attack on a number of occasions in recent years, there is no area of Canadian life where leadership is more positively endorsed.

It's not that Canadians think the police are perfect. On the contrary, since 1975, less than 40% have agreed that *"law enforcement is applied evenly to all those who break the law,"* including a low of 16% in 1990. Today's level is 25%.

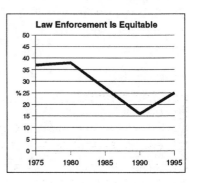

Law Enforcement Is Equitable

Even if most people don't believe that policing is always fair, a majority nonetheless still believe that this is one area of Canadian life where, ultimately, they can have confidence.

Canadians don't, however, feel the same about the court system. We increasingly may be willing to create a society where people are treated fairly and justly. But since the 70s, we've consistently believed that the courts haven't been tough enough with law-breakers.

• Some 85% have been maintaining *"the courts do not deal harshly enough with criminals."*

• About 80% have been saying *"the death penalty should be exercised in some instances."*

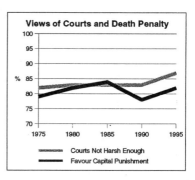

Views of Courts and Death Penalty

Courts Not Harsh Enough
Favour Capital Punishment

There is an extremely high level of uniformity among Canadians concerning the police, the courts, and capital punishment.

• Differences between *women* and *men* and *younger* and *older* Canadians are small.

• *Regionally*, people living in B.C. are especially critical of law enforcement. Support for capital punishment is somewhat lower in Quebec and margin-ally higher on the Prairies.

Nationally, criticism of the courts and support for the death penalty are both up a little from 1990.

Views of the Police, Courts, and Capital Punishment

	LAW ENFORCET EQUITABLE	COURTS NOT HARSH ENOUGH	FAVOUR CAPITAL PUNISHT
CANADA	25%	87	82
BC	13	92	81
Prairies	22	87	88
Ontario	29	87	85
Quebec	29	86	75
Atlantic	24	88	82
Women	22	88	81
Men	29	87	83
18-34	25	88	78
35-54	25	87	83
55+	26	90	85

PROJECT CANADA FAST-FACTS

Our aversion to law-breakers, such as sex offenders and people who have spent time in prison, can be seen in the following comparisons.

"Would feel uneasy around a person, initially knowing only that the person is . . . "

	A Known Sex Offender	A Drug Addict	An Ex-convict	An Alcoholic	A Former Mental Patient	A Person With AIDS
1995	95%	83	81	64	62	61
1985	**	76	72	52	70	**
1975	**	77	71	60	67	**

Politicians

Life for politicians, the surveys show, is something of a roller-coaster.

• In 1975, 61% of Canadians were saying that Pierre Trudeau was doing "a pretty good job as Prime Minister," and 65% were applauding our political and economic system. By just 1980, only 44% were happy with Trudeau's performance, and the applause for the system had died down to 53%.

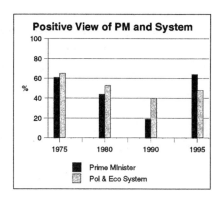

Positive View of PM and System

Prime Minister
Pol & Eco System

• As noted earlier, in 1990, a mere 19% of the populace were satisfied with what Brian Mulroney was doing, and support for our political and economic system had slid all the way to 40%. Just five years later, Jean Chrétien is receiving cheers from 64% of Canadians, and endorsement of the system has rallied back to almost 50%.

In light of our clearly articulated desire to experience "the good life," complete with economic well-being, it's hardly surprising that we get impatient very quickly with politicians who we see as messing up our financial situations.

In the post-1960s, the pattern has been clear.

• We are quite willing to personally pursue what we hope for relationally. When we look to government, we are concerned first and foremost about economic matters.

• Governments that have been perceived to be top-heavy with agendas such as bilingualism and multiculturalism (the Liberals of Trudeau), or unity and constitutional reform (the Conservatives of Mulroney), have been fairly decisively dismissed.

PROJECT CANADA FAST-FACTS

Here's how people have described their own "political views (not party)."

	BC		Prairies		Ontario		Quebec		Atlantic	
	1975	1995	1975	1995	1975	1995	1975	1995	1975	1995
Extremely Liberal	5%	7	2	2	3	5	7	11	2	6
Liberal	26	23	18	23	27	22	27	32	23	18
Moderate	58	54	45	48	48	52	63	52	50	57
Conservative	10	14	33	24	20	19	3	4	20	18
Extremely Conservative	1	2	2	3	2	2	0	1	5	1

Overall, we hardly are a country that holds our politicians in high esteem. The findings are pretty conclusive.

• We have *limited confidence* in politicians, be they federal, provincial, or local, with 45% of us going so far as to say that government incompetence is a "very serious" national problem.

• More than 60% of us think our politicians have *too much power*, in sharp contrast to average Canadians.

• We think politicians are making far *too much money* – sort of like professional athletes, lawyers, and dentists.

• And, despite our power to elect and remove politicians, over half of us don't really think we *"have any say about what the government does."*

It doesn't add up to a particularly pretty picture. By the way, we'd also like to get rid of the Senate.

The Media

In the post-1950s, television and other media forms have assumed an increasingly prominent role in our lives.

On a day to day basis, the media inform and entertain us, stimulate and soothe us. They help us to cope with reality and, when we so choose, provide us with alternate realities. Few Canadians can go – or do go – very long without "a media fix." We've "gotta have" that paper or program or experience.

The media know. Thanks to ever-advancing technology, the media options and their accessibility have only accelerated with time. The diverse possibilities of print, sight, and sound today are succinctly summarized in the multimedia computer, a glorious machine that offers us a geometric jump in entertainment and communication, putting us in touch with the entire world . . . complete with sight and sound . . . in seconds . . . from the comfort of our own homes.

A quick glance around us reveals that we are making a lot of use of a lot of different information and entertainment mediums.

Use of Media Forms

	DAILY	SEV TIMES A WEEK	ABOUT ONCE WEEK	2-3 TIMES MONTH	ABOUT ONCE A MONTH	HARDLY EVER	NEVER	TOT
Music	70%	18	5	3	2	2	<1	100
Television	66	21	10	<1	<1	2	<1	100
Newspapers	50	23	16	3	2	5	1	100
Computers	33	14	5	3	3	14	28	100
Books	30	20	8	10	14	16	2	100
Magazines	11	27	23	16	12	8	3	100
Internet	10	5	3	2	1	10	69	100
Videos	3	9	20	23	18	18	9	100
Movies	0	1	4	8	17	58	12	100

Yet, we seem to have a love-hate relationship with the media. We're also confused about the media's impact.

• While we readily access its available forms, we're quick to emphasize that we're not really *influenced* all that much by the media – "we make up our own minds."

• We also say we don't have much *confidence in* the media, less so as we go from radio and newspapers (40%) to TV (30%) and movies (20%).

Perception the Media Have Excessive Power

BC 65 Prairies 68 Ontario 62 Quebec 47 Atlantic 51

• But, in the next breath, we say the media have far "too much power" and we are frequently concerned about the negative effects they are having on our children and teenagers, and – come to think of it – on our society as a whole.

Many Canadians seem to think that there is at least one reliable media organization – the CBC.

At a time when the role of the public network is being seen by some as passé, some 64% maintain *"CBC television continues to play a unique role in enhancing Canadian culture."*

• Such positive senti-ments are shared quite evenly across Canada, and by ma-jorities in every re-gion – even by a slight majority of Quebec francophones (53%) with respect to "La télévision de Radio-Canada."

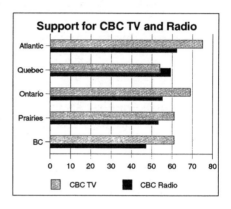

In addition, 55% of Canadians *do not* agree that *"CBC radio programs would be better under private ownership."*

• *Regionally*, CBC radio support increases as one moves eastward.

• *Age-wise*, there is virtually no difference among adults in their support for CBC TV and radio.

CBC Support by Age

	TV	Radio
Nationally	64%	55
18-34	66	46
35-54	62	42
55+	62	46

The Longer Look
Gallup put the same question about CBC radio programming to the nation in the late fall of 1942. Of those with a definite opinion, 71% did not feel CBC radio programming would be better under private ownership.

121

TREND TRACKING

The caution and suspicion that we frequently display in our interpersonal dealings are being extended to our institutions. We are extremely fussy customers who exhibit little time and patience with leaders and organizations that don't serve us well.

And the mood of most of us is that we are not being served particularly well by anyone, except the police. We're often frustrated with educators, the courts, politicians, the media, religious leaders, labour unions, and just about everyone else. Ironically, at the same time we say we are happy people who place particular value on life in Canada.

Especially during times of intense change and economic instability, it's important for people to know who can be counted on "out there." For many, the police are one of the few "dependables." Rapid change in our vaguely defined culture also leaves us with few symbols of cultural stability. The CBC may be among the very few.

One of the former dependables whose place is unclear as the century winds down is the subject of our last chapter.

THE PROJECT CANADA PANEL			
	NO CHANGE	NOW AGREE	NOW DISAGREE	TOTALS
Have a say in what the government does			
Baby Boomers	58%	16	26	100
Boomers' Parents	63	12	25	100
Capital punishment			
Baby Boomers	80	9	11	100
Boomers' Parents	84	8	8	100

10 - REDEFINING RELIGION
What We Don't Want and Want

*"If the Church is ailing, it is
certainly worth reviving."*
-Pierre Berton

1965	Vatican II concludes in Rome. RC churches celebrate mass in English. Pope reaffirms opp to birth control. Berton publishes *The Comfortable Pew*.
1970	Anglican and United Churches experiencing losses after mid-60s highs. Pentecostals claim significant gains. Church relinquishes educ in Quebec.
1975	Anglicans accept women as priests. Speculation many turning to cults. Jamaican Rastafarians investigated by Toronto metro police.
1980	Lois Wilson becomes the first woman moderator of the United Church. Ontario govt releases study of cults and sects carried out by Daniel Hill.
1985	Supreme Court rules Lord's Day Act unconstitutional. United Church embroiled in debate over homosexuality. De Roo call for native self-govt.
1990	Scandal and abuse seems rampant. Nine-month Mount Cashel probe ends. Ontario court rules public school religion courses may violate Charter.
1995	Mainliners downsizing. Scientols lose suit. Graham comes to Skydome. Church-run educ ending in Nfld. Faith grps seek recognition of holy days.

**One of Canada's institutions that has been affected most
by the social changes of the post-1950s is religion.**

Many of the country's groups are in serious trouble.

- Participation is down sharply.
- Confidence in religious leaders has tumbled since the 1970s.
- Religion's influence seems to be peripheral.

Yet, there are signs that religion is hardly being abandoned.

- People are holding an amazing range of supernatural beliefs.
- Large numbers say they have spiritual interests and needs.
- Some 9 in 10 continue to identify with religious groups.

There also are indications that the decline in religious participation is having some important consequences for Canadian life.

• Religious groups historically have given much emphasis to interpersonal values, such as civility and compassion. Declining participation has meant such values have been losing a key proponent. It's not clear yet who's picking up the slack.

• The quest for spirituality continues. But, relatively few people appear to be turning to alternatives to traditional religion.

Organized Religion

I have been tracking and chronicling religious trends now for some time. The patterns are fairly straightforward.

• Our earliest information suggests that, around 1945, some 60% of Canadians were attending religious services just about every week.

• As late as the mid-60s, about 75% of Catholics and 25% of Protestants were still attending on close to a weekly basis.

With the 1970s, a sharp decline in attendance began to occur that particularly affected Roman Catholics in Quebec and, across the rest of the country, so-called "Mainline Protestants" – the United, Anglican, Presbyterian, and Lutheran churches.

• As of the mid-90s, about 25% of Catholics in Quebec claim to be weekly attenders, compared to around 40% of Catholics in the rest of Canada.

• Some 20% of Canadians who identify with Mainline Protestants say they are weekly churchgoers – close to the same level estimated for people identifying with "Other Faith Groups."

124

Two religious group bright spots exist.

• *Outside of Quebec, Roman Catholics* still constitute a large and fairly involved church.

• *Conservative Protestant* groups – Baptists, Pentecostals, Alliance, Mennonites, Salvation Army, and Nazarenes, for example – know both high involvement and, collectively at least, numerical growth.

Weekly Service Attendance 1975 Through 1995			
	1975	1985	1995
NATIONALLY	31%	28	25
ROMAN CATH	45	37	30
Quebec	49	31	24
Outside Quebec	41	40	38
MAINLINE PROT	23	16	19
Anglican	24	16	17
United Church	28	13	20
CONSERV PROT	40	60	64

On the surface, *United and Anglican Mainliners* look like they now are holding their own and maybe even rebounding, especially since the mid-80s. The problem is that the census tells us that the two groups' "affiliate pools" – people who identify with them – have shrunk significantly since the 70s, from 18% to 12% of the population in the case of the United Church, and from 12% to 8% in the Anglican instance.

The Longer Look

* Research on teens today indicates about 18% are weekly attenders and 11% place a high value on religious involvement. The 1995 survey has found that 86% of Canadians feel *"teenagers are not as interested in religion as they were 25 years ago."*

* Gallup put the same question to the nation in the summer of 1955. At that time, 66% of Canadians said that teens weren't *"as interested in religion"* as they had been *"25 years ago."*

Between 1975 and 1995, some important changes have been taking place.

• Attendance is still highest in the Atlantic region (near 40%).

• Catholic attendance continues to exceed Protestant attendance in every region of the country.

• But despite its Atlantic high – similar to the situation in an industrializing Quebec a decade or so earlier – the Catholic attendance in the Atlantic provinces has fallen significantly since the 70s. Catholic attendance in the region is now similar to the Protestant level.

• Protestant weekly attendance has remained fairly steady at about 25% west of Quebec.

Attendance by Region

	1975	1995
BC	**18%**	**21**
Catholic	41*	25*
Protestant	15	24
PRAIRIES	**27**	**30**
Catholic	37	36
Protestant	28	31
ONTARIO	**27**	**24**
Catholic	44	38
Protestant	23	25
QUEBEC	**35**	**19**
Catholic	41	24
Protestant	29*	**
ATLANTIC	**52**	**38**
Catholic	76	46
Protestant	38	41

*Sample size small, % unstable. Included for heuristic value.

The relationship between community size and attendance has changed very little since the 70s for Protestants.

• But largely reflecting the Quebec and Atlantic declines, Catholic attendance is down in every size of community.

• Here, as with region, there's a tendency for Catholic attendance to fall to around "the Protestant plateau"; such convergences are to be expected in highly secularized societies.

• Protestants continue to have their strongest proportional support in smaller cities and towns; community size does not have much effect on Roman Catholic involvement.

Attendance by Community Size

	1975	1995
Over 400,000	26%	22
Catholic	59	31
Protestant	23	22
100,000-400,000	27	19
Catholic	60	22
Protestant	25	28
10,000-99,000	33	21
Catholic	56	29
Protestant	20	20
<10,000	39	31
Catholic	48	34
Protestant	33	37

What has to be most disturbing for religious groups, however, is the news about age structure. Younger adults today are less likely to be involved in groups than their counterparts of two decades ago. As a result, many religious groups are increasingly top-heavy with older people.

With the inevitable aging of the population, it's clear that things are going to get worse before they get better in many and probably most group instances.

The best demographic evidence available through Statistics Canada indicates that Protestant Mainliners, along with Roman Catholics in Quebec, will be experiencing nothing less than dramatic numerical losses over the next twenty years.[1]

By the year 2015, we will be looking at a drastically revised

N.B.

By the year 2015, we will be looking at a drastically revised Canadian religious landscape.

• *Mainliners* will be on the sidelines; the formerly marginalized *Conservative Protestants* will form the new Mainline.

• *Roman Catholics* will remain very prominent nationally, but will experience a large loss of active people in Quebec.

• *Other faith groups*, faced with the debilitating impact both of acculturation generally and intermarriage specifically will find it difficult to sustain numbers, let alone grow.

Current and Projected Weekly Attenders
In 1000s

	NOW	2015
NATIONALLY	**4,600**	**3,500**
ROMAN CATH		
Outside Quebec	1,500	1,200
Quebec	1,200	550
MAINLINE		
Anglican 220	100	
Lutheran	80	50
Presbyterian	80 →	75
United Church	400 →	200
CONSERVATIVE		
Baptist	200	225
Other	740 →	900
OTHER FAITHS	200	175

From: Bibby, *Unknown Gods*, 1993:106.

PROJECT CANADA FAST-FACTS

Respondents were asked in the 1995 survey what they think their immediate response would be if they found themselves in a situation where the only thing they knew about a person was that he or she is a "a born-again Christian."

* Some 70% said "at ease," 24% "a bit uneasy," 6% "very uneasy."
* Uneasiness ranged from 37% for those under 35 to about 25% for both Boomers and Boomers' Parents.

128

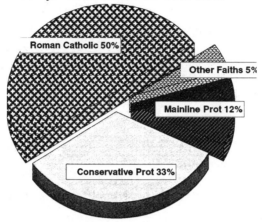

Weekly Attenders in the Year 2015

Roman Catholic 50%

Other Faiths 5%

Mainline Prot 12%

Conservative Prot 33%

The Alternatives

In view of the post-60s decline in service attendance, I have been keeping an eye on possible alternatives that people might be adopting. **To date, there's little evidence that sizable numbers of Canadians who are not involved with traditional groups are actually turning elsewhere.**

• In the 1970s, some observers were assuming that many people were interested in a number of so-called "new religious movements."

• The 1975 survey found little support for such a claim, especially among the people who supposedly were turning to such movements as options to traditional Christianity.

"Strong Interest" In New Religions	
1975	
Transcendental Meditation	5%
Children of God	3
Zen	2
Hare Krishna	<1
Satanism	<1
1980	
Any new movements	
Presently	2
In the past	3

• In 1980, only small numbers of people indicated an interest in *any* new movements.

At the time, the most commonly cited "new group" was "TM," which many regarded not as a "religion" but as a practice often engaged in by people with conventional religious leanings.

• In the late 1980s and 1990s, considerable publicity has been given to the New Age movement. New Age books, music, practices, and personalities – from Shirley MacLaine through John Denver – have become fairly well-known.

• The 1990 and 1995 surveys have explored Canadian interest in the movement. But here again, the proportion of people who are saying that they are highly interested is not very large and, to date, is not increasing. The number who move on to involvement is even smaller.

Interest in the New Age Movement			
	STRONGLY INTERESTED	INVOLVED IN Activities	Groups	Networks
1990	3%	3	2	2
1995	3	3	2	<1

Beliefs and Practices

The decline of organized religion and the limited success of alternative expressions is occurring at a time when conventional and less conventional beliefs and practices are flourishing across the country.

Fairly traditional beliefs and practices, for example, have remained quite stable since the 70s.

• A solid majority of Canadians continue to believe in *God,* the *divinity of Jesus,* and *life after death,* including heaven. Certainty of belief in God is down slightly, but the percentage of people who say that they actually don't believe in God was about 3% in 1975, 10% in 1985, and 8% in 1995.

• But a majority also hold beliefs some of us didn't think were particlarly common in the 90s – that *miraculous healings* occur; in *angels*; and, yes, even in *hell*.

Conventional Beliefs
"Definitely" or "Think So"

	1975	1980	1985	1990	1995
God	89%	85	83	82	81
Mirac healing	**	**	**	**	74
Div of Jesus	71	69	79	75	72
Life after death	73	69	65	68	71
Heaven	**	**	**	70	67
Angels	**	**	**	**	61
Hell	**	**	**	46	49
Experienced God	47	43	44	43	43

• Sizable numbers of Canadians also report that they are *praying privately*, saying *table grace,* and are *reading the Bible* or some *other Scriptures.* In fact, only 1 in 4 say they "never" pray privately. The levels have been stable or have increased since 1975.

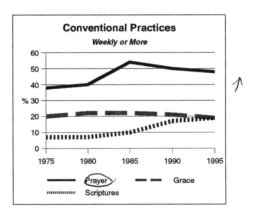

PROJECT CANADA FAST-FACTS

Canadians indicating they watch religious programs on TV at least occasionally, versus seldom, or never:

1975 - 59% ; 1980 - 46%; 1985 - 21%; 1990 - 18%; 1995 - 18%.

What's more, many Canadians continue to hold a wide array of less conventional beliefs, although the levels have tended to waver somewhat over the past twenty years.

• More than 7 in 10 people indicate that they believe in *near-death experiences*, while about 6 in 10 express belief in *ESP*, and that some individuals have special *psychic gifts* of prediction.

Less Conventional Beliefs
"Definitely" or "Think So"

	1975	1980	1985	1990	1995
Near-death experiences	**	**	**	**	74
ESP	73%	70	60	59	55
Psychic powers	**	59	63	59	56
Exper precognition	**	59	55	47	49
Spirit world contact	**	**	**	39	43
Astrology	49	45	35	34	34
Will be reincarnated	**	**	**	24	27
Communicatn with dead	38	**	21	23	25
Know astrological sign	**	**	**	90	88
Read horoscope *Daily*	14	12	12	13	10
Never	23	25	33	**	31

• Half think they have personally experienced *precognition*.

• Canadians also have a high level of openness toward ideas about death: more than 40% think we can have *contact with the spirit world*, 25% that we actually can *communicate with the dead*; 1 in 4 say they personally expect to be *reincarnated*.

• One in 3 continue to give credibility to *astrology*; most know their signs and read their horoscopes at least occasionally.

The Longer Look

Intrigue with a wide range of topics regarding the unknown is pervasive.

* In the spring of 1950, Gallup found that 12% of people across the country maintained that "flying saucers are from other planets."

* In 1995, 46% of Canadians believe "some UFOs are from other planets."

As might be expected, there are some variations by age and education.

• Younger adults are inclined to embrace a wide range of both conventional and less conventional beliefs.

• People with university degrees are slightly less inclined to hold beliefs; nonetheless, the differences are relative: those with more education have not exactly abandoned the gods.

	GOD	LIFE AFTER	MIRAC HEALING	NEAR-DEATH	SPIRIT WORLD	WILL BE REINCARN
Select Beliefs by Age and Education						
18-34	78%	77	72	79	52	29
35-54	81	68	75	76	45	27
55+	85	66	75	63	25	22
A degree/more	74	66	72	74	40	21
Post-secondary	84	71	75	77	47	30
HS or less	85	74	76	72	42	29

Spirituality

In recent years, the American media have led the way in claiming that large numbers of people who are not particularly interested in organized religion are nonetheless searching for ways to meet their spiritual needs. Interest in spirituality is said to be high.

Some observers in Canada have assumed that what is true for the Americans is true on this side of the border as well.

I've attempted to explore the interest in spirituality in the 1995 survey, and to understand its relationship to organized religion.

• About 35% say that *"spirituality" is* "very important" to them, 30% that it is "somewhat important."

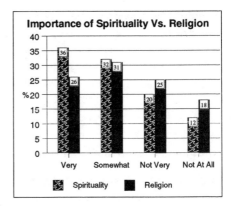

Importance of Spirituality Vs. Religion

• The corresponding figures for religion are roughly 25% and 30% respectively.

• In addition, asked about *trends over "the past five years,"* 22% of Canadians report that there has been an increase in their interest in *spirituality*, while just 9% say the same for their *attendance* at religious services.

• And asked pointedly, *"Do you have spiritual needs?"*, some 52% across the land say they do, 48% that they don't.

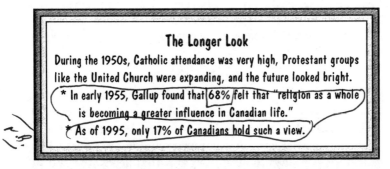

The Longer Look

During the 1950s, Catholic attendance was very high, Protestant groups like the United Church were expanding, and the future looked bright.

* In early 1955, Gallup found that 68% felt that "religion as a whole is becoming a greater influence in Canadian life."
* As of 1995, only 17% of Canadians hold such a view.

So what does all this mean?

To begin with, **the 25% of the population who are actively involved in groups are considerably more likely than others to say they have spiritual needs, highly value spirituality, and have become more interested in spirituality in recent years**. That's especially true of Conservative Protestants.

Spirituality Interest and Organized Religion				
	Have Spiritual Needs	Highly Value Spirituality	Highly Value Religion	Increasing Interest in Spirituality
NATIONALLY	**52%**	**36**	**26**	**22**
Weekly	78%	75	74	40
Monthly	56	30	18	17
Yearly	40	18	7	14
Never	31	24	4	19
Roman Catholic	52	35	26	21
Mainline Protestant	49	33	24	17
Conserv Protestant	84	73	63	49
Other Faiths	71	57	51	40
None	41	26	2	19

However, that said,

• large numbers of people who are *not highly involved* in religious groups do indicate that they have spiritual needs and that they place a high value on spirituality; *N. B.*

• these people include perhaps 25-30% of those 5 million Canadians who say that they *"never" attend* religious services, and around 25-40% of those 2 million people who say that they are not affiliated with any religious group.

Does the Attendance Drop-off Matter?

To look at a number of our findings through the eyes of religious involvement is to find that, generally speaking, there are fairly small differences between people who are actively involved in religious groups and other Canadians.

• Weekly attenders tend to exhibit pretty much the same characteristics – "good and bad" – they are just as likely to be happy, pro-Canadian, and to worry about their kids.

• They are no more negative about visible minorities nor less inclined to engage in sex. Partly reflecting age, "weeklys" are somewhat less likely to report having been sexually assaulted.

Select Characteristics by Service Attendance

	HAPPY	FAMILY ENJOYT	VALUE CDN	VISMINS TM POW	SEX WEEKLY	WORRY CHILDREN	SEXUALLY ASSLTED
Weekly	96%	97	67	17	74	52	7
Monthly	91	90	64	12	75	45	10
Yearly	91	93	57	18	79	50	15
Never	89	89	58	21	77	35	10

Such findings suggest the attendance drop-off is not associated with significant differences in the **quality of life** of Canadians. Religious involvement undoubtedly helps to enhance life for many people. But others seem to be finding alternative sources to involvement which likewise enhance life for them.

Can the same be said for **interpersonal values**? The findings suggest that in many instances – *friendliness, kindness, politeness* – the answer is yes. However, there are some noticeable differences in the case of traits like *honesty, concern for others,* and, in particular, *generosity* and *forgiveness*.

Alternative sources of values are apparent. Still, it's worth noting is that in no value instance are weekly attenders *less likely* than others to endorse these traits. At minimum, religious groups appear to be a major source of interpersonal values.

Select Values by Service Attendance

	FRIEND- LINESS	KIND- NESS	HONESTY	POLITE- NESS	CONCERN OTHERS	GENER- OSITY	FORGIVE- NESS
Weekly	78%	83	95	73	77	68	71
Monthly	67	81	90	67	67	58	55
Yearly	64	73	86	63	63	54	49
Never	76	83	85	73	69	49	53

Even though many Canadians are not actively involved in religious groups, they show an uncanny inclination to not abandon the country's dominant religious groups. Identification without involvement tends to be the norm.

The Meaning of Religious Identification
by Service Attendance

	ALL	WEEKLY	MONTHLY	YEARLY	NEVER
Grew up in this tradition	79%	81	83	79	64
Know a fair amount about my group's tradition	70	90	71	60	46
Group I identify with is important to me	61	88	72	40	15
Currently very involved	27	74	19	2	3
Would describe myself as "deeply committed"	37	79	33	14	4
Would consider being more involved if worthwhile for myself or my family	62	69	69	58	43

Still, to the extent they can find that their identification groups can play a significant role in their lives or in the lives of their family members, large numbers of people – including those not currently participating – indicate they are receptive to the possibility of greater involvement.

The Longer Look
* Just 35% of the 1995 respondents could identify *Revelation* as the last book in the New Testament.
* But wait – in 1955, during the alleged Golden Era of attendance, Gallup found that only 33% of Canadians could name the book!

Onlookers outside of Canada's religious groups seldom greet the numerical problems of organized religion with much concern, let alone alarm. However, it seems almost prosaic to point out that two of the most basic functions that Canadian religious groups have performed historically pertain to *values* and *spirituality*.

Involvement meant that large numbers of children and adults were at least introduced to the importance of traits such as honesty, compassion, and generosity. In the 90s, with service attendance dropping, there is reason to believe we have not yet found equally effective alternatives. Perhaps significantly, these days many are concerned about issues such as teen crime, violence in schools, and violence against women and children.

As for spirituality, it's clear the number of Canadians who express needs readily exceeds the number involved in organized religion. While it's often assumed people will simply turn else-elsewhere or turn inward, many appear to be doing neither.

The decline of organized religion in the last half of this century is socially tragic if equally effective sources of civility and spirituality fail to appear. To date, their arrival is in question.

THE PROJECT CANADA PANEL			
	NO CHANGE	INCREASE	DECREASE	TOTALS
Attendance				
Baby Boomers	33%	43	24	100
Boomers' Parents	37	39	24	100
Private Prayer				
Baby Boomers	33	49	18	100
Boomers' Parents	45	39	16	100

CONCLUSION

The survey findings indicate that life as we have been experiencing it since the 1960s has been characterized by a blend of change and continuity, diversity and commonality.

• We've been doing a lot of changing but, as the panel findings remind us, we've also been holding on tightly to ideas and behaviour we value.

• We've become more aware of our geographical, cultural, and lifestyle differences, yet, a well-kept secret is that we also have continued to have much in common.

Change and Diversity

The surveys document considerable change in the past few decades, not just collectively but individually as well. Many of those changes reflect an increasing openness to diversity – to a wide range of people and how they choose to live.

• We've made considerable progress in the way we **view each other**. Gender and intergroup relations have improved considerably since the 70s. There's still a good distance to go. But we have come a long way from where we were.

• **Sexually**, we've been showing a willingness to accommodate people whose attitudes and behaviour are not necessarily our own, be they heterosexuals or homosexuals, be the topic birth control or abortion.

• We've been exhibiting openness to a wide range of **family** possibilities – from being divorced, blended families and single parenthood, through cohabitation and having children outside of marriage, to being more accepting of same-sex couples.

- Our **entertainment** and **sports** inclinations have become even more American-oriented than in the past. Television and aggressive marketing have heightened our awareness of U.S. sports and, when the Americans have given exposure to established Canadian sports such as hockey and figure skating, have raised their profiles and enhanced their stars *in this country*, apart from what has been accomplished states-side.

- We've also been changing in the way we view our **institutions** and **leaders**. A greater level of individualism, more choices, and limited resources have combined to make us increasingly demanding. We expect solid performances from people who influence our lives. If we're not happy, we'll remove a politician, bypass the local school, or ignore the church. In succinct marketing jargon, "the customer is king." N.B.

Continuity and Commonality

Change and diversity, however, tell only half the story. Continuity and commonality tell the other half.

- We're not changing all that much when it comes to probably the most practical question we bring to our society: **what we want out of life**. We want to be happy and free, and look to relationships and economic well-being to get there.

- We also haven't changed very much when it comes to our **personal** and **social concerns**. We don't think we have enough money or time, worry a fair amount about our health, and never seem to stop worrying about our kids. Our primary social preoccupations are finding jobs – which we think are diminishing – and not having to worry about crime and violence – which we think are on the rise.

- While we're not always sure about other people, we continue to put a lot of importance on **interpersonal traits** such as honesty and reliability, friendliness and concern for others.

Of primary importance, diversity has been oversold and commonality undersold. Regardless of where we live and who we are, when it comes to our wants and our concerns, we Canadians have a tremendous amount in common.

I'm not so sure we know it. **Geography, self-serving politicians, and an opportunistic media have often functioned to keep us apart.**

• People outside of Quebec, for example, consistently have maintained that French Canadians have too much power in Canadian life. Francophone Quebeckers feel just the opposite.

• Yet the surveys show that, since at least the 70s, average Quebeckers have been saying they have limited interest in the unity question or French-English relations. What concerns them first and foremost is the economy, and jobs.

• Sound familiar? It should. People in Alberta and Ontario and B.C. and Nova Scotia have been among those telling the pollsters the same thing for years.

Quebec is distinct in so many ways. However, Quebeckers are not "distinct" when it comes to what they want from life. If they ever "opt out," ironically, it will be because they want what the rest of us want – but think they may have a better chance of getting them without us.

Some Final Reflections

So here we are as the century winds down – pretty content with life as a whole, but fairly upset with where we seem to be going financially. The economic dissatisfaction in Quebec leaves average people there highly vulnerable to new possibilities. To the extent the federal government is perceived as being out of touch with economic needs, in time others could follow.

Some things are easy to predict – concern about the economy and crime will be primary . . . half of the Boomers will have retired before they hit 65 . . . those who move elsewhere will be heading for Vancouver, just as Gallup found people were doing way back in 1945 . . . a unique culture will persist in Quebec . . . the rest of Canada, having decided not to have *"a* Canadian culture," will – led

PROJECT CANADA FAST-FACTS

"Will gain influence by the year 2000"

	1975	1985	1995
Science	80%	83	77
Education	55	56	46
The traditional family	15	32	29
Traditional morality	20	28	24
Canada	68	54	37
The United States	22	47	37
Europe	22	18	33
The United Nations	22	24	24
Russia	38	30	17

by Toronto and the Toronto-based national media – fill much of the void with American culture . . . outside of Quebec, cultural domination by the U.S. will mean that only the most powerful and most isolated parts of Canada "will survive" culturally – all major pro sports will be limited to Toronto, Montreal, and Vancouver, while "Canadian subcultures," complete with local heroes and histories, will persist in the more remote parts of the country Canada . . . in a strange "Canadian way," Quebec's every move will be anxiously monitored, while the cultural house is being looted.

Strange we had so little interest in cultivating Canada . . . the CBC, Mounties, and CFL seem to be about all "the rest of us" can call our own. Don't get me wrong – our culture won't be a bad thing, just a borrowed thing. But then again, maybe there's hope. If Quebec can do it, maybe we can, too.

APPENDIX

The book is based primarily on the adult data collected as part of what has evolved into *The Project Canada Research Program* at The University of Lethbridge. National surveys of adults 18 and over have been carried out in 1975, 1980, 1985, 1990, and 1995. Complementary surveys of youth have been completed in 1984, 1988, and 1992.

Data Collection. All five of the adult surveys have made use of self-administered questionnaires and have been conducted by mail. Questionnaires have ranged from eleven to twenty pages in length, and have included 300 to 400 variables. The goal has been to generate extensive information on life in Canada, with specific attention given to social issues, intergroup relations, and religion. With minor variations, the procedures have involved (1) mailing the questionnaire with a front-page cover letter, (2) sending a follow-up postcard, and (3) mailing a second questionnaire. Surveys typically have been carried out over a four-month period.

Sampling. A representative sample of about 1,100 cases is sufficient to claim a confidence level of 95% and a confidence interval of four percentage points when generalizing to the Canadian adult population.

Size and *representativeness* are the two key criteria in being able to generalize with accuracy from a sample to a population. Considerable care therefore has been taken to ensure that both standards have been met. Concerning size, an interest in provincial comparisons resulted in 1,917 cases being gathered in 1975, 1,482 in 1980, 1,630 in 1985, 1,472 in 1990, and 1,713 in 1995. With respect to representativeness, the nation has been stratified by province (ten) and community size (>100,000, 99-10,000, <10,000), with the sample drawn proportionate to the populations involved. As resources have improved, the number of communities being drawn on has increased from 30 in 1975 to 43 in 1980, 104 in 1985, 145 in 1990, and 228 in 1995. Participants have been randomly selected using telephone directories. Discrepancies between the sample and population characteristics have been corrected by weighting for provincial and community size, along with gender and age. Each of the five samples has been weighted down to about twelve hundred cases in order to minimize the use of large weight factors (i.e., three or more).

As can be seen in TABLE A1, all of the samples are highly representative of the Canadian population. Samples of this size and composition, as noted, should be accurate within about four percentage points on most questionnaire items, 19 times in 20 similar surveys. Comparisons with similar Gallup poll items, for example, have consistently found this to be the case.

The Panels. A major interest of the ongoing national surveys has been to monitor social change and stability. Each survey sample since 1980 has consisted of (a) a core of people who participated in the previous survey and (b) new participants, who are used to create a full national sample of about 1,500 cases. For example, while the first 1975 survey was a typical cross-sectional survey with 1,917 participants, the *PROJECT CAN80* sample of 1,482 people included 1,056 who had also been involved in 1975.

The 1995 sample of 1,713 cases includes 916 people who participated in previous surveys and 797 new cases. Of the 916, a total of 400 participated in the 1975 survey. They are comprised of the ongoing core who have participated in all the surveys (230) and a special panel supplement (170), which was obtained through our adding as many of the original 1975 participants as we could whom we had "lost" between 1980 and 1995.

TABLE A1. Population and Sample Characteristics: 1975 Through 1995 (In %'s)

	1975 Pop	1975 Samp	1980 Pop	1980 Samp	1985 Pop	1985 Samp	1990 Pop	1990 Samp	1995 Pop	1995 Samp
Community Size										
100,000+	55	55	51	52	52	54	53	53	53	54
99-10,000	13	13	15	15	15	16	15	15	15	14
<10,000	32	32	34	33	33	30	32	32	32	32
Gender										
Female	51	50	51	49	51	50	51	51	51	50
Male	49	50	49	51	49	50	49	49	49	50
Age										
18-34	39	37	43	40	41	42	40	38	37	35
35-54	35	36	31	31	32	33	33	35	36	38
55+	26	27	26	29	27	25	27	27	27	27
Marital Status										
Married-Cohab	70	69	67	67	66	65	67	67	66	66
Never married	22	18	23	20	24	23	21	18	20	20
Widowed	7	10	7	10	6	7	6	7	8	6
Divorced	1	3	3	3	4	5	6	8	6	8
Education										
Post-Secondary +	35	39	41	48	46	50	51	55	58	62
Secondary or less	65	61	59	52	54	50	49	45	42	38
Ethnicity										
British	45	49	43	**	40	46	42	50	44	49
French	28	20	28	**	27	29	31	26	29	28
Other	27	31	31	**	33	25	27	24	27	23

Population source: Statistics Canada. **Not available.

Realizing a total of 400 was possible, we set that figure as our quota goal; hence the even number. These 400 are the people who comprise what I call "The Project Canada Panel" in the book. They have been weighted for gender. While no claim is being made that the panel members are representative of all

Canadians, they collectively provide intriguing and novel data on the attitudes, outlooks, and behaviour of a core of Canadians over a twenty-year period.

Return Rates. For national surveys, the *PROJECT CANADA* return rates have been relatively high – 52% in 1975, 65% in 1980, and about 60% in 1985, 1990, and 1995. We tend to hear from some 65% of the people who have participated previously and just over 50% of those being contacted for the first time. Incidentally, the seldom-reported cooperation rates that researchers obtain in face-to-face and telephone interviews is typically around 65% – occasionally higher, often less.

Funding. The 1975 survey was carried out for a cost of about $14,000 and had four major sources: the United Church of Canada ($2,000), the Canadian Broadcasting Corporation ($3,000), the Solicitor General of Canada ($5,000), and the University of Lethbridge ($4,000). In 1980, the panel portion of the survey was made possible by grants from the Social Sciences and Humanities Research Council of Canada ($10,000) and the United Church of Canada ($2,000). The second phase of *PROJECT CAN80*, which involved filling the core out into a full national sample, cost approximately $8,000 and was funded primarily by the University of Lethbridge. *PROJECT CAN85* was funded completely by the Social Sciences and Humanities Research Council of Canada ($45,000). *PROJECT CAN90* and *PROJECT CAN95* were both funded by the Lilly Endowment (about $65,000 each).

Complete methodological details concerning the complementary *PROJECT TEEN CANADA* surveys that I refer to from time to time can be found in Bibby and Posterski, *Teen Trends*, pages 321-324.

NOTES

INTRODUCTION

1 Berger, Peter L. *Invitation to Sociology*. New York: Doubleday, 1961.

CHAPTER 1/ Reaffirming Happiness

1 In national surveys involving 4,000 teenagers carried out in 1984 and 1992, colleague Don Posterski and I found that some 90% of 15 to 19-year-olds said that freedom is *"very important"* to them. That figure was matched only by the value placed on *"friendshi."*
2 From 1980 onward, the surveys have included an item asking respondents to estimate whether there has been *"an increase,"* *"a decrease,"* or *"no particular change"* in a number of areas of life, including *"your general happiness."*
3 In the analysis here and following, "Boomers" are being viewed as 35 to 54-year-olds, "Boomers' Kids" as 18 to 34, and "Boomers' Parents" as those 55 and older. The cutting points are somewhat arbitrary but are fairly consistent with standard definitions of Boomers. They also result in the generation of three samples of sufficient sizes to permit reasonably accurate generalizations to these three age cohorts.
* Gallup Polls   Women employed – November 18, 1942; happiness – June 4, 1960.

CHAPTER 2/ Rethinking Enjoyment

* Gallup Polls   Leisure, 1945 – March 24, September 6, September 26, movies, 1948; weather – April 30, 1955; sports – February 4, 1942.

CHAPTER 3/ Reevaluating Values

1 See Reginald W. Bibby and Donald C. Posterski, *Teen Trends*. Toronto: Stoddart, 1992:98.
* Gallup Polls   Salaries – November 25, 1950.

CHAPTER 4/ Recreating Culture

1 Bibby, Reginald W. *Mosaic Madness*. Toronto: Stoddart, 1990:7.
2 See Bibby and Posterski, *Teen Trends*, 1992:60-69.
3 The same pattern holds for young people in Quebec, especially francophones, versus teenagers elsewhere. See Bibby and Posterski, 1992:119-123.
* Gallup Polls   Preferred country – June 8, 1960; 1950, favourites – June 7, 1950; First Prime Minister, Ottawa – June 27, 1945; President – May 9, 1945; national anthem – August 9, 1950; Grey Cup – November 23, 1955; greatest living Canadian – August 26, 1942.

CHAPTER 5/ Reworking Relations

* Gallup Polls   Immigration good – August 2, 1950; immigrant as neighbours – November 26, 1955; crime increasing – September 6, 1950.

CHAPTER 6/ Reexamining Sexuality
1 For a profile of "religious nones" in Canada, see Reginald W. Bibb
  Unknown Gods. Toronto: Stoddart, 1993:37-50.
2 For details on teenage sexuality, see Bibby and Posterski, 1992:37-50.
3 See Bibby and Posterski, 1992:40-43.
* Gallup Polls   Sex education – September 1, 1943.

CHAPTER 7/ Revitalizing Individuals
1 See, for example, M. Scott Peck, *The Road Less Traveled.* New Yor
  Simon and Schuster, 1978.
2 Gwynn Nettler. *Social Concerns.* Toronto: McGraw-Hill, 1976:10.
3 In 1980, health was regarded as so obvious that it was not included in t
  list of concerns. I have taken the liberty to list it here as one of the top fi
  concerns. It has been a concern option in all of the other surveys, with r
  1980 assumption about its importance documented.
* Gallup Polls   Euthanasia – May 31, 1950; bedtime – May 2, 194
               physicians and dentists – August 30, 1950; ideal numb
               of children – November 28, 1945.

CHAPTER 8/ Readdressing Issues
1 The exact figures: good talking to 39%, taking away privileges 31'
  being grounded 12%, physical discipline 10%, other 8%.
* Gallup Polls   Women drivers – November 19, 1955; social issues
               October 10, 1945, May 28, 1955; teenagers acting up
               April 2, 1955, 1965; home discipline – March 30, 1955, Ju
               7, 1965; disciplining teenagers – April 6, 1955; curfew
               August 7, 1965.

CHAPTER 9/ Reassessing Leadership
* Gallup Polls   Teachers – April 29, 1950; the RCMP – May 27, 195
               speed traps – August 24, 1955; capital punishment
               October 6, 1943; Senate – August 31, 1942; CBC radio
               November 21, 1942.

CHAPTER 10/ Redefining Religion
1 For details, see Bibby, 1993:96-109.
* Gallup Polls   Teenagers 25 years ago – September 17, 1955; flyi
               saucers – June 17, 1950; religion's influence – Februa
               19, 1955; Revelation – September 21, 1955.

CONCLUSION
* Gallup Polls   Vancouver – February 17, 1945; Canada breaking up
               January 20, 1945.